Parenting and Child Resilience in Disadvantaged Communities

**Available
in alternative
formats**

This publication can be provided in alternative formats,
such as large print, Braille, audiotape and on disk.
Please contact: Communications Department,
Joseph Rowntree Foundation,
The Homestead, 40 Water End, York YO30 6WP.
Tel: 01904 615905. email: info@jrf.org.uk

Parenting and Children's Resilience in Disadvantaged Communities

Peter Seaman, Katrina Turner,
Malcolm Hill, Anne Stafford, Moira Walker

national
children's
bureau

JOSEPH ROWNTREE
FOUNDATION

Joseph Rowntree Foundation

The Joseph Rowntree Foundation has supported this project as part of its programme of research and innovative development projects, which it hopes will be of value to policy-makers, practitioners and service users.

National Children's Bureau

NCB promotes the voices, interests and well-being of all children and young people across every aspect of their lives. As an umbrella body for the children's sector in England and Northern Ireland, NCB provides essential information on policy, research and best practice for its members and other partners.

NCB aims to:
■ challenge disadvantage in childhood
■ work with children and young people to ensure they are involved in all matters that affect their lives
■ promote multidisciplinary, cross-agency partnership and good practice
■ influence government through policy development and advocacy
■ undertake high-quality research and work from an evidence-based perspective
■ disseminate information to all those working with children and young people, and to children and young people themselves.

The views expressed in this book are those of the authors and not necessarily those of the National Children's Bureau, the Joseph Rowntree Foundation or the University of Glasgow.

Published by the National Children's Bureau for the Joseph Rowntree Foundation

National Children's Bureau, 8 Wakley Street, London EC1V 7QE
Tel: 020 7843 6000.
Website: www.ncb.org.uk
Registered Charity number 258825

NCB works in partnership with Children in Scotland (www.childreninscotland.org.uk) and Children in Wales (www.childreninwales.org.uk).

© University of Glasgow 2005

Published 2005

ISBN 1 904787 70 3

British Library Cataloguing in Publication Data
A catalogue record for this book is available from the British Library

Contents

List of figures

List of Tables

Introduction

This report is based on two linked studies, which examined the experiences and perspectives of parents and children living in disadvantaged communities in the west of Scotland. These investigations were part of a programme of research funded by the Joseph Rowntree Foundation on parenting and understanding children's lives. The two studies were conducted separately and with differing timescales, but the same key themes were explored in both and participants were from the same areas. The analysis was coordinated and the writing-up blended findings from both pieces of research. This report is also informed by a separately funded literature review on parents and resilience (Hill and others 2004).

The studies occurred at a time when parenthood and the behaviour of young people were receiving considerable policy attention. This was exemplified by measures ranging from the establishment of a National Family and Parenting Institute to the introduction of Parenting Orders as one means of responding to anti-social behaviour (ASB). Also area-based strategies for dealing with disadvantage (reclassified as social exclusion) were once again prominent (for example, Education Action Zones in England, certain Social Inclusion Partnerships in Scotland).

The focus of the research was to explore how 'ordinary' families manage parent–child relationships during the middle childhood in adverse environments. The participants in the research were chosen because they lived in areas that scored highly on indices of material deprivation. Yet, in keeping with the thrust of the overall programme, the intention was to have a 'normative' sample that would cover, as far as possible, a broad range of families who were by and large coping. This reflected the aim of the studies to highlight the strengths and strategies of parents and children for promoting the well-being of the children and keeping them safe, in the context of their perceptions of hazards in their local areas.

The research was informed by ecological perspectives on children's development and needs (Bronfenbrenner 1979; Jack 2000; Horwath 2001). Different elements of children's lives are seen as crucially influenced by characteristics of their parents, neighbourhood and broader social processes – not singly but interactively. The ecological approach can fruitfully be enhanced with concepts from social network theories and from current debates about social capital. These emphasise how social connections may compound material and educational difficulties or offer support, models and pathways to overcome disadvantage (Trevillion 1999; Morrow 1999; Putnam 2000; Baron and others 2000; Hill 2002, 2003). Similarly research and concepts within the resilience framework emphasise how key informal network members and individual professionals can be crucial in enabling children to recover from early adversity (Fonagy and others 1994; Gilligan 1997, 2001). It is essential, however, that parents and children are not seen simply as passive recipients of environmental influences, since they have opportunities to exercise choice, even when faced with major life constraints. This is a key tenet of social construction approaches to children and childhood (James and Prout 1998).

For the purposes of the studies, a disadvantaged community environment was defined as one characterised by high levels of unemployment, crime and illegal drug use. It is difficult for any one study to encompass a wide range of parental stages or children's ages, so the research concentrated on children aged eight to 14 and parents of such children. This is the stage at which significant increases typically occur in the amount of time children spend beyond the close supervision of home and school (Collings and others 1995).

The parenting study lasted for two years. Its objectives were to describe:

- what parents consider to be the main threats to their children's safety and well-being
- how parents seek to protect their children and minimise the effects of these threats, acting both as individuals and in interaction with other family members, social networks, community groups and/or professionals such as teachers
- the diversity in parents' views and actions, while also identifying common elements which derive from the fact that they live in a poor neighbourhood.

The children's study began six months later and took place over 18 months, with objectives to investigate:

- children's views and experiences of their local community
- children's expectations and wishes with regard to their daily activities
- children's aspirations for the future
- what children consider to be the main opportunities and threats to fulfilling their expectations, wishes and aspirations

- what children regard as the main threats to their safety and well-being and how they cope with these
- children's understanding of parental and adult concerns about their safety and well-being
- children's perspectives on the strategies, rules and guidance their parents use in seeking to protect their children.

The next chapter discusses relevant literature and then details of the study design and samples are given. Subsequent chapters present the findings and conclusions.

1. What we know from previous research

Children and families living in disadvantaged communities

When the present government came to power around one-third of children in the UK lived in poverty. The government pledged in 1999 to eradicate child poverty in Britain within 20 years, an ambition since adopted by the Scottish Executive, which aims to eliminate child poverty 'within a generation'. Recent figures show child and family poverty decreasing but not at a rate observers or the government would like (Bradshaw and Mayhew 2005; NCH 2004). It is not poverty alone that disadvantages children now and their future prospects, but the interplay between experiences of family low income, financial insecurity and prevailing lifestyle expectations (Wilkinson 1994).

Parents living on low incomes deploy a range of money-management strategies to help them cover their costs, but also tend to give priority to expenditure on children (Middleton and others 1995; Backett-Milburn and others 2004). Children, too, may mask or suppress their needs and wants in order to reduce the pressure on parents, while older ones sometimes engage in paid work to assist with family finances (Ridge 2002).

The present studies explored not the experience of living in poverty *per se* but the experience of living in communities characterised by high levels of disadvantage. Broad economic and social factors affect poverty and social exclusion, but local communities are also the containers of resources and obstacles to achieving expectations in terms of lifestyle and employment (Pierson 2002). There has been a long-standing tendency for inequalities of income and wealth to be reflected in spatial divisions, with people on low incomes tending to be restricted to living alongside others who are also materially disadvantaged in 'marginalised areas' with limited environmental assets (Byrne 1999; Glennerster and others 2004). Parents living in such 'poor environments' tend to experience multiple stresses and have high levels of physical and mental health problems (Ghate and Hazel 2002).

The region in the west of Scotland where this research was conducted encapsulates many of the factors surrounding relative disadvantage and includes many poor environments of varied character, though in parts of these local people regard their quality of life as good (McKendrick 1995). The region has an emerging post-industrial economy in which the opportunities for young people are very different from those their parents had a generation or so ago. The transition to adulthood has changed, with a premium put on education and the learning of transferable skills for opportunities in a growing service sector.

Children's agency and resilience

In planning the studies, the authors saw it as vital to include children's perspectives. Children are not simply the products or recipients of parenting, but contribute actively to the creation of their own family and extra-familial lives (James and Prout 1998). Indeed they can be skilful in exploiting weaknesses or divisions in parental relationships and rules in order to garner more control for themselves over their activities and use of space (Valentine 1997, 2004). Children living in poverty do experience many restrictions as their parents cannot afford to pay for the same level of material goods or activities as others, but also develop their own ways of seeking to ameliorate the effects of limited resources, in which friendships can play a crucial part. However 'they are also engaged in intense social and personal endeavour to maintain social acceptance and social inclusion' (Ridge 2002, p. 141). Children are also adept at identifying risky people and situations, as well as using strategies to minimise threats (for example, by avoiding them or by not being alone) (Harden and others 2000).

In recent years both research and professional practice have been affected by the emergence of a strengths-based approach to hardship (Saleebey 2002). Although not exclusively confined to the experience of economic hardship, the resilience perspective can be helpful in gaining insights into how people in high-risk communities negotiate the balance of opportunities and barriers to successful parenting and growing up. Resilience has been defined variously, but the main element is an ability to do well despite adverse conditions (Gilligan 2000; Fonagy and others 1994; Howard and Johnston 2000). For the most part, resilience research and theory have been examined in relation to children. Some have focused on family

resilience (for example, McCubbin and others 1999), but very little attention has
been given to the notion of parental resilience.

Resilience has been a guiding theme for the present studies, as it can focus on
individual characteristics within the context of family networks and processes and is
conceived as an interactive process between an individual or family and features of
their environment (Hill and others 2004). A broad inventory of factors has been
identified that may insulate against challenges to growing up satisfactorily that arise
in circumstances of disadvantage. These include family environments characterised
by warmth, responsiveness and stimulation; provision of adequate and consistent role
models; harmony between parents; spending time with children; promoting
constructive use of leisure and community networks; consistent guidance and
structure and rules during adolescence (Gilligan 2001; Hammen 2003; Rosenthal
and others 2003). Firm application of rules and detailed awareness and control of
children's whereabouts appear particularly valuable in protecting children from the
adverse effects of growing up in poor neighbourhoods, whereas more flexible
parenting is generally deemed preferable in lower-risk environments (Baldwin and
others 1990; Titterton and others 2002).

Parenting and community

Borland and others (1998) explored parents' perceptions of the hazards and dangers
faced in their communities. Parental fears and degree of felt security were shaped by
location. For example, parents living in suburbs saw them as comparatively 'safe' in
terms of exposure to busy roads or crime and delinquency, so their worries were
mainly focused on outside threats, like 'stranger danger'. In housing schemes, the
dangers were more tangible and identifiable with risks stemming from local gangs
and neighbours. In a similar manner, Hood and others (1996) also revealed that risk
perceptions were gendered. Parents expressed concern that girls were at risk of
becoming adults 'too quickly', whereas worries about boys more often related to
dangerous outside activities and pressures from peer groups.

There is a relationship between perceived risk and parental discipline styles. One of
the best-known classifications of parental style remains that of Baumrind and Black
(1967) who identified 'authoritative' parenting as the desirable ideal, characterised
by warmth and expression on behalf of the parent but also a regard for children's
growing cognitive abilities to establish rules for themselves. Authoritative parents lay
down defined boundaries for children and punish transgression but allow children
to share the thinking behind parental policy. Maccoby and Martin (1983) reviewed

subsequent research to show that emotionally warm, firm but flexible discipline was associated with better outcomes for children in arenas such as scholastic attainment and self-esteem, compared with the other styles (authoritarian and laissez-faire) identified by Baumrind and Black.

Laybourn (1986) examined parenting style in poor neighbourhoods. She found children who resisted getting into trouble in high-risk areas had parents who held them accountable, expected them to do more at home and acted fast if they were worried about their children's associations. In a later study, supervising children as closely as possible was again reported as the strategy most favoured by parents in a deprived urban setting (Borland and others 1998). This time-consuming approach meant that parents could deal with issues as they arose, such as protecting their children if they encountered immediate risks. These risks were often close to home. Suburban parents by contrast were more likely to encourage unsupervised play and worry about the effects of being overprotective. Suburban parents could also utilise *preparation* to a greater extent. Preparation involves helping children manage the risks on their own with support and guidance from their parents, alerting children about risks and giving them 'survival skills' and strategies when faced with dangerous situations. The place of discussion and surveillance in parents' disciplinary and keep-safe strategies was central in the present study.

Families' interactions with the wider community

Long before the recent development of the resilience perspective, pioneering community studies had attempted to locate the strengths within socio-economically poorer communities (for example, Bott 1957; Wilmott and Young 1957). Many of the positive elements highlighted in these studies have since been included within the concept of social capital, which encompasses the resources and trust available in social networks (see Introduction).

The nature and frequency of interactions between families living in the same neighbourhood affects the availability of support and the extent to which standards of behaviour are shared or enforced (Coleman 1988). In particular children tend to accept parental authority more easily when the expectations of other adults around them are similar (Fletcher and others 1995). Similarly, parents are usually more willing to allow their children greater freedom of movement when they know and trust the parents of their children's friends (Seaman 2003). By contrast, if people living in the same area do not associate much with each other, then they are less likely to agree about what behaviours are acceptable or take coordinated action to prevent or respond to problems. For instance, the Joseph Rowntree Foundation's *Communities in the Balance* report (Page 2000) describes an 'estate culture' in some marginal communities characterised by a tolerance of crime, drugs and anti-social behaviour, an acceptance of low personal and educational achievement, compounded by strong peer pressure to conform to these expectations. This leads to the development of negative social capital at both individual and community level. Individuals may lower their personal and educational aspirations in order to fit in, and those who have high aspirations become marginalised or move on. Holman (1998), however, states that powerlessness and lack of investment is associated with negative stereotyping. He argues that research should recognise the strengths of people living in poor communities, as well as their problems and needs.

Ghate and Hazel's (2002) recent study assessed the balance of support and stress stemming from living in disadvantaged communities. They found parents described their areas as friendly and stable, with informal support coming predominantly from locally based female relatives. However, it was feared that requesting help too often would be interpreted by others as a failure to cope. Moreover, while access to informal support networks was a beneficial form of social inclusion for those involved, it could be experienced as excluding. Minority ethnic parents, lone parents and those living in the most deprived areas reported fewer informal supports.

Family diversity and change

Dixey (1999) has argued that responsibility for keeping children safe still rests mainly with mothers. Despite the increase in the proportion of women working and the emergence of new masculine identities in the last few decades, the majority of childcare and supervision tasks are still carried out by women. The patterns become complicated as mothers are more likely not only to occupy multiple roles as mother, spouse and employee, but trends in family formation have increased the likelihood of fathers being non-resident. Seaman (2003) has shown how elements of non-resident partners' or ex-partners' inputs can be viewed as a positive contribution to child rearing when the relationship between parents facilitates and supports this. Although there is nothing inherently problematic for children raised in lone-parent households, these are more likely than others to be in poverty. Single mothers in lower socio-economic positions often experience financial strains, negative life events and inadequate support (Simons 1996).

Family life has been affected increasingly by commercial and peer pressures for conformity as regards material possessions (for example, with respect to children's clothes and technological equipment). At the same time young people's educational and employment opportunities and decisions have become more individualised, but with those brought up in poverty least well equipped to take advantage (Furlong and Cartmel 1997).

Conclusions

This chapter has briefly reviewed evidence from earlier British research. Several themes have emerged, which were explored further in the present study with an emphasis on the strengths deployed by parents and children to respond to the challenges of living in disadvantaged communities. These themes include:

- the close interaction between low income and living in marginalised neighbourhoods
- how parenting, supervision and discipline are shaped by parents' aspirations, children's responses and community values
- the linkages between intra-household communication and levels of trust and support in local social networks.

2. Design of the studies

The studies were planned to be primarily qualitative, so they would draw on participants' own definitions and priorities, recognising the 'pluralization of [their] life worlds' (Flick 1998, p. 2). Samples of parents and children were accessed via schools.

Data-gathering methods

Focus group discussions were used to facilitate interchanges, openness and flexibility (Hennessy and Heary 2005), while individual interviews were favoured for exploring personal experiences and views more fully. A small number (seven) of the children's interviews included two siblings, as they preferred this. A range of techniques was used to stimulate discussion and anchor conversation in particular situations (for example, vignettes, picture prompts, brainstorming).

At the same time, it was seen as helpful to be able to generalise quantitatively about certain key opinions and aspects of parent–child relations, so questionnaires were distributed to parents and children via schools. The questionnaire for young people was specially devised to be interesting (for example, with pictures and tick boxes), while covering similar topics to those in the parent questionnaire.

The interview and discussion schedules, as well as the questionnaires, were developed to include questions related to each of the main themes identified in the studies' objectives, notably:

- perceptions of the immediate and wider neighbourhood: positive and negative, supports and risks
- children's activities
- parents' and children's keep-safe strategies

- responses to worrying or scary situations
- family rules and discipline
- network relationships
- hopes and aspirations, opportunities and obstacles.

A short-term parental advisory group was established to give guidance about the precise questions to be asked and manner of presenting them.

Access and sampling

On the basis of official data about unemployment and poverty, four study areas were selected to give a range of socio-economic environments. In this report these have been given disguised names:

Inner city – Yardinch
Outer estate – Newhouse
Old industrial town – Foundry
New town – Greenparks

Families were accessed via school, to give a cross-section of the community, although individuals and families with major problems may have declined to take part. In each area, one secondary and an associated primary school with high rates of free school meals agreed to take part.

Initially contact was made with parents to take part in the parenting study. Questionnaires were sent to parents via schools. At the end of the questionnaire was an invitation to take part in an interview and a focus group discussion. The questionnaire was quite long and the response rate low. In order to boost the number of complete questionnaires, a wider population of parents in the same schools and in two other schools in the same areas were invited to complete questionnaires. Overall the response rate for questionnaires was one-quarter (26 per cent).

Later, a sub-sample of the parents interviewed were asked if they and one of their children of the appropriate age would agree for the children to be interviewed individually to provide complementary data to that of their parents. However most of the children for the focus groups and interviews were recruited separately. As the questionnaire required a certain level of literacy and understanding, it was distributed only to young people in secondary school (first and third years).

The achieved samples for both studies are shown in the tables below:

Table 2.1 Details of parent study samples

Individual interviews	84
Focus group discussions	17
Completed questionnaires	227

Table 2.2 Characteristics of parents from questionnaires

Gender	60 males		171 females
Household	Living with partner		162 (71%)
	Living alone		53 (23%)
	Living with other person		12 (6%)

The number of households surveyed was 193; in 34 households questionnaires were returned from both parents (or parental figures). This means that in tables based on the questionnaires, the totals for individual views includes some double counting of households.

Ethical issues

Ethical approval was obtained from the University of Glasgow Faculty of Social Sciences Ethical Committee. Care was taken to provide clear and attractive information sheets to assist with obtaining informed consent from both parents and children. Confidentiality was promised, unless a situation of serious harm was revealed.

Table 2.3 Details of children's study samples

Individual interviews	60
Focus group discussions	16
Completed questionnaires	259

Table 2.4 The age and gender of children interviewed

Gender	28 males	39 females
Age	27 aged 8–10 years	40 aged 11–14 years

(N = 67)

Coding and analysis

With agreement, the great majority of interviews were tape recorded and transcribed. Transcripts were coded and analysed using the software packages N5 and N-VIVO to identify and develop key themes. The data from the questionnaires was coded and entered into SPSS for analysis.

3. Children's and parents' perceptions of their local area

The starting point for the study as a whole and for particular interviews concerned the different opinions that parents and children held about their local neighbourhoods. In particular they were asked about the good and bad features of where they lived, the 'risky' and safe places.

Perceptions of the local area

Both parents and young people described good and bad aspects of their local areas, and this chapter attempts to reflect the balance as reported. Positives and negatives usually related to the presence of trusted or threatening people (and their behaviours) and less often to features of the built environment (such as traffic). For both adults and young people the extent and proximity of 'risks' such as violence, substance misuse and anti-social behaviour affected their lives in crucial ways and considerably shaped parents' family management styles. Although risk was mainly embodied in the threatening actions of individuals or groups, often respondents were aware of the factors such as poor housing and unemployment that underlay the behaviour. For instance, they characterised risky areas in terms of dilapidated housing.

Parents and children did not define the whole community as safe or unsafe, but they recognised certain places within the areas that were risky. Interestingly, these places were often public facilities such as parks and sports facilities that could in other circumstances be seen as offering opportunities for young people. When they talked of the positive aspects of their communities they emphasised that relative safety was offered by being known, knowing nearby residents well and the related community spirit.

Differentiation of area and territoriality

Parents and children talked about their area in a very localised way. Early qualitative work revealed perceptions were fine-grained, so this was taken into account when devising the questionnaire. Parents and children were asked to tell us about first the immediate *local* area they lived in (their streets or 'scheme') and secondly the *wider* area. The survey showed how in three of the areas more parents rated their immediate *local* area as excellent, than did so for the wider study location (Table 3.1). The new town, Greenparks, did not follow this pattern.

The propensity to 'talk up' the immediate local area is illustrated by respondents in Newhouse, where only 8 per cent of parents rated this as 'bad or really bad' whereas a quarter of respondents described the wider area in this way. In interviews this local comfort zone was explained as resulting from good knowledge of immediate areas so they felt better equipped to deal with issues of risk and safety, together with the reassuring presence and support of familiar people:

> The neighbours are lovely. I cannot say anything about my neighbours. As I say, we've got a few drug addicts in the street but they don't really bother us in any way whatsoever. The neighbours across the road, they'd do anything to help you. I mean when you're at work during the day they'll take your bins out for the bin men coming and they'll put the bins back in and, you know, just wee niceties like that, they'll look after your house if you're away on holiday and things like that. If you run out of milk you can always go in and ask one of your neighbours sort of thing. No they're very nice, I can't say anything about my neighbours, basically. (*Mother, Newhouse*)

The quotation above shows how trust among neighbours not only resulted in mutual assistance, but also diminished the impact of proximity to illegal drug misuse.

Table 3.1 How do you rate your area as a place to bring up children?

	Newhouse (%) N=39		Greenparks (%) N=44		Foundry (%) N=64		Yardinch (%) N=24	
	Local	Wider	Local	Wider	Local	Wider	Local	Wider
Excellent	10	3	19	26	14	3	13	4
OK	53	42	60	58	58	62	50	33
Neither good nor bad	29	30	19	12	25	30	21	43
Bad/really bad	8	25	2	4	3	5	16	5

Consequently, parents could also become very loyal to their immediate areas and rely upon the familiarity and support they received from people nearby to help them parent effectively. In Newhouse in particular, some parents would not think of living elsewhere within the larger scheme on the basis that they liked their current neighbours and saw them as vital source of support. However, there were also differences in the physical environment and social fabric so that some local areas were perceived as much more desirable places to live and bring up children:

> We stayed over in the towers and there's a big difference in Rachael from when she moved over here, she goes out to play now, she's sociable now whereas before she was just stuck in the tower over the road like a hermit, she just wouldn't go out of the door, she would go into the lifts, wouldn't do anything ... she's got friends over here, you'd never see her out by herself. They've got a swing park and a big field down there, they've got a glen where they take the wee dog. It's really a better environment over this side of the road than it is over the other side, because it's all concrete over there. I mean they call it a concrete jungle because it is all garages and car parks, there's nothing for kids over there. (*Mother, Foundry*)

As well as differentiation of local spaces, there was also temporal differentiation of the same space. Some areas that were seen as safe during weekdays became threatening to both adults and children in hours of darkness or at weekends. This was linked to the kinds of people present and the activities they engaged in at such times, with consumption of alcohol and drugs raising the perceived risks at various times.

When young people in the questionnaire survey were asked to rate their area they mainly responded 'average' (55 per cent) or 'good' (32 per cent). A somewhat higher proportion than adults reported it as being 'poor' (11 per cent). From a standard list of features about their area they might like, young people mainly referred to their social networks and facilities: 'having friends nearby' (72 per cent), 'easy to get around' (70 per cent), 'having good neighbours' (56 per cent), 'good housing' (52 per cent), 'lots of shops' (50 per cent) and 'good schools' (48 per cent). Many fewer selected 'it's safe' (34 per cent), 'it's quiet' (28 per cent), 'plenty to do' (27 per cent) or 'clean' (24 per cent). These figures suggest that for young people as well as parents, people were the main strength in their areas. It is also notable that few said there was plenty to do.

When asked what was bad about their area, young people's replies highlighted behaviour by other people, notably 69 per cent citing 'gangs' as a problem and 66 per cent the related issue of graffiti. 'Dirt and litter' was chosen by 65 per cent and 'nothing to do' by 63 per cent. 'Drugs' and 'people who might hurt you' were both chosen as issues in their area by 46 per cent of young people and 'crime' by 42 per cent. In Newhouse, the figure for drugs rose to 58 per cent.

When asked if children and young people get into trouble in their area, 88 per cent said 'yes'. The things they got into trouble about are listed below (Table 3.2). Most of this involved aggression to people or property, but it is noteworthy that the seemingly neutral activity of hanging around the streets was reported as the second most common type of 'trouble'.

Just over half thought boys were more likely than girls to get into trouble and most of the rest thought gender made little difference (Table 3.3).

Table 3.2 Reasons why young people get into trouble

Reason for getting into trouble	n (ticked)	%	Rank
Fighting other people	203	89	1
Hanging around the streets	193	85	2
Vandalising	195	86	3
Drinking alcohol	190	83	4
Fighting in gangs	180	79	5
Making a lot of noise	177	78	6
Smashing windows	161	71	7
Starting fires	151	66	8
Annoying the police	141	62	9
Playing fireworks	130	57	10
Stealing	99	44	11
Doing drugs	75	33	12
Trouble for doing nothing	70	31	13
Getting pregnant	31	14	14

(Respondents could tick on a standard list as many reasons as they thought applied)

Table 3.3 Are boys or girls more likely to get into trouble?

More likely to get into trouble	N	%
Boys	124	56
No difference	97	44
Girls	4	2

(Responses to multiple choices on questionnaire)

Youth gangs

As we shall see later, children's friendship groups were key to children's well-being and sense of safety, yet when they took the form of gangs, peer association evoked concern or fear among both adults and children in the studies. In interviews and discussions, references to gangs were prominent in the ways young people explained their movements and activities in their neighbourhoods (see also Table 3.2). Ideas about gang territoriality influenced where both parents and children felt safe and were able to go without anxiety. The widespread concern about youth gangs expressed by young people and parents is the negative flipside of the safety experienced from having knowledge of, and identifying with, local areas. Gangs were associated with small localities, some corresponding to the local areas to which respondents felt they belonged. Gang territories were defined by groups of streets within larger schemes (estates) or had definite physical boundaries (such as a bridge over the motorway in Newhouse). In some instances, gang names had even become synonyms for a particular housing scheme or 'end' of a housing scheme. Families felt relatively safe in their own immediate areas, either because it was not regarded as a gang territory or because gang hostility was usually directed at young people from outside, as indicated by the young respondent below:

> If I am going to another area obviously I watch myself because there is young lassies oot there and boys that think anybody from another scheme is a total outsider, d'you know what I mean? I've seen it happen before in front of my very eyes ... gangs going up and gawn 'You're no' fae here', 'So whit ye dae'ing here?' and then they start fighting. So if I go to another place I'll always, I'm no' frightened or anything, but I always watch myself.
> (*14-year-old girl, Yardinch*)

This shows how heightened caution, if not avoidance, was required in relation to passing through territories adjacent to one's own, but where one would be seen as an outsider ('no' fae here').

Gangs and territoriality were not simply features of present youth subculture. Many of the gang names and territories had remained the same from when parents were young, and still informed their understanding of the local area and of safe and unsafe places. When parents referred to gangs therefore, many were not simply talking about groups of young people who merely appeared threatening to adults, but are drawing on their own childhood experience of real threats. Parents told how the notion of gang territory restricted young people's freedom of movement so that not being recognised as coming from a certain area would increase the potential for being picked on:

> Aye, aye, a lot of them get hassled but I've not had that problem because my boy doesn't go out the scheme anyway. The furthest he goes is to the back of the shops where there's a five-a-side football pitch, that's all, he just goes down there, he doesn't go out. (*Mother, Newhouse*)

Conversely, being recognised within one's own area by gang members enhanced the relative safety of that area according to children and some parents. However, it was a form of safety that most parents did not appreciate, since they believed that being known to 'the wrong crowd' readily led to getting drawn into trouble with them.

When comparing the accounts given in each of the four areas, it appeared that gangs were more of a phenomenon for young people in Newhouse and Yardinch. The Newhouse young people described their local gangs as consisting mainly of boys aged 13 to 17. They referred to several gangs and, like the parents, identified each with a particular name and a specific scheme. There were reports that individuals from different areas fought one another, with conflicts usually starting when individuals from one scheme crossed into another. The gangs were described as fighting most weekends, usually at territorial boundaries. One young person from Newhouse commented that gangs fought at the weekend because that was mostly when teenagers drank. Some interviewees knew individuals who had been stabbed and a few knew, or knew of, people who had died in gang fights. Although it was commented that most of the fights only involved gang members, many children thought there was always a risk of becoming caught up in the trouble, and so best not to go near the places where fights occurred. Interviewees suggested that gangs would attack anyone they did not recognise, reinforcing the link between recognition and safety. In Yardinch, a similar picture emerged to that in Newhouse, including the importance of alcohol use as a lubricant for gang activity, particularly at weekends:

> It's maistly at the weekend because everybody's had a wee drink o' the gallus watter! The drink. Everybody feels dead game ... as if they could conquer the world when they have a drink so that's mainly the time ... like they are all dead bold and naebody will kill me! D'you know what ah mean that's maist of the time they'll fight ... cos they've all got a wee drink in them. (*14-year-old girl, Yardinch*)

Threats posed to safety by alcohol and drug users

It was not only other young people who posed threats to children and constricted their movements. Potential exposure to alcohol and drug use by older residents also placed limits on where young people and their parents felt safe. In the quote below, a father relates the prevalence of alcohol abuse to social exclusion (lack of employment opportunities for young adults) and illustrates how it could create a threatening atmosphere:

> The only thing I think that's bad about the area is like – you know, the guys that are maybe not working, the ones from sort of 16 to about 20 or something, they stoat about the streets drunk and shouting, I don't know, singing football songs. And it's when these people are all behaving like that, that's when people are getting stabbed and they're getting into fights and – I suppose there's a lot of alcohol problems in the area, I would say. (*Father in group interview, Newhouse*)

Such problems could also restrict access to facilities such as parks, sports and leisure facilities that might otherwise be seen as offering developmental advantage or foster independence. They could also make moving around local areas more hazardous, whether on foot or by public transport.

> From a parent's point of view, I no longer feel completely happy about you [addressing her child] moving about because there are a lot of other young people taking drugs and they're a dodgy lot as far as picking on you and trying to snatch mobile 'phones away from you. And even the buses, I don't feel particularly happy if you're going on a bus yourself because of the trouble and the stabbings and things that you hear, the violence. And then of course you've got the perverted kind of people and you've got the drunks, that's another thing I worry about, there are a lot of people that have a drink problem. (*Mother, Greenparks*)

Some parents, such as the mother above, introduced ideas about dangers from paedophiles but it was clear that threats from those misusing alcohol were larger in the minds of most parents than that of sexual abuse. The latter was a much more concrete risk since many parents and young people had witnessed drunkenness or the effects of drugs first-hand within their communities. Heroin and 'jellies' – licensed tranquillisers available on the black market – caused the most concern. One of the threats that could be associated with drug use was theft. The ubiquity of mobile phones, which parents generally saw as facilitating safety, could actually increase young people's vulnerability to theft.

Alcohol or drugs were often cited as being used mainly in particular areas of schemes or locales. These places were likely to be characterised by poorer-quality housing that local housing associations found difficult to let, creating what many parents saw as a cycle of decline as 'bad families' were more likely to make up incoming residents. It was commonly reported in Newhouse, Foundry and Yardinch that a street's decline was marked by an influx of drug-using tenants into local rented housing stock. Some parents were aware of individual houses that were occupied by a drug user or dealer. They felt that people coming and going to buy drugs, with the possibility of coming into contact with their children, was a problem. Certain other spaces such as shops, buses or open spaces could bring young people close to drugs or alcohol use, so parents would be wary of their children being near there.

Young people too, identified less safe areas by their association with adults using alcohol in public or drug taking. Part of this fear was that alcohol and drugs were seen to make people aggressive or unpredictable:

> And their eyes are pure wild and they are just look to you like that. There's people like, see round our bit, there are a lot of nice people round there, and they are nice and kind to you. But like some, see when they have like a drink in them and they will get like angry and shouting.
> (*Group 8, 10-year-old girls and boys, Newhouse*)

While the predominant view of drunken behaviour was negative, it could also be treated as entertainment. A 14-year-old girl bemoaned the presence of drunken arguments and fights in a nearby area, but also said she and her friends went to witness and provoke 'drunks' as 'it's a good laugh'.

Another group remarked on how in a given location, the degree of safety or risk was dependent on the time of day and week, and on who was there:

> Well it is like in the morning, people like old people 'cause they are polite and like people who are pregnant and with prams and everything. But at night when they get drunk and there is violence and everything. And at the weekend the chippie is open and they are off. Especially sometimes on a Sunday. They want to get to their place quick and it is like road rage and everything ... in the morning they are all right, but at night they are crazy.
> (*Group of 12-year-old boys, Greenparks*)

Children also avoided drug and alcohol users because of fears of being attacked, infected maliciously by needles or stolen from. They could back these fears up with concrete accounts of such incidents happening to themselves, family or friends in the past. Individuals of all ages referred to areas where teenagers or adults drank or took drugs, and described how there were discarded needles and smashed bottles in parks, tunnels or stairways. This implied that drug and alcohol issues affected all children's personal safety and daily lives. Certainly some of the interviewees' accounts indicated that such issues were very close to home and made even the immediate area unsafe.

> See my brother he was walking home from school one day, but he's left school now, and he was walking up there a lane at my bit so you can walk through there quicker. And there were these drug addicts standing and they jumped him to get his money so they could get their drugs, but he had to fight back and so he fought them and then his pal came over and he had a mobile so they phoned the police and they arrested the two guys.
> (*Group 3, 12-year-old boys, Foundry*)

Accessing facilities: issues of known and unknown places

The questionnaire asked about facilities parents and their children had access to in the local and wider areas (Table 3.4). Though the majority had access to a park in their local area, many did not. Many people in Newhouse and Greenparks said they had an indoor sports facility close by, which was more rarely the case in Foundry and Yardinch. Far more residents of Greenparks and Foundry said they could access commercial leisure facilities in their wider area than in Newhouse and Yardinch.

A regular complaint from parents was of there being little for young people to do in the areas in which they lived, even though some reported their children having

Table 3.4 What facilities do you have access to?

	Newhouse (%)		Greenparks (%)		Foundry (%)		Yardinch (%)	
	Local	Wider	Local	Wider	Local	Wider	Local	Wider
Park	51	54	61	64	77	64	71	38
Indoor sports facility	62	65	73	75	25	59	38	50
Sports club	31	48	48	73	13	42	21	33
Other club	33	33	34	50	17	30	29	4
Commercial leisure	8	38	23	89	31	73	17	46
Other space	35	33	57	64	50	52	4	21

(Figures show percentage of parents who indicated that the facility was available in their local or wider area)

hobbies and activities. Further questioning revealed that not uncommonly parents did know about a service within reasonable distance, but were reluctant for their children to use it, because of concerns about possible attacks or intimidation by gangs or drunken/drugged adults. This was exacerbated when a family did not have access to a car, because using public transport was seen as increasing exposure to risk of attack and itself representing an unsupervised space.

In Newhouse, two-thirds of questionnaire respondents had an indoor sports centre in their *wider* area, but this was sometimes treated as out of bounds in the minds of respondents, because going there would entail passing through a gang territory or gang members might pose a threat at the centre itself. These points are illustrated below:

> The kids have got a lack of amenities, there's nothing for them to do. There's a wee church and that's one day a week, that's it, there's nothing. I mean they cannae go – I mean those lassies were saying about territorial, that is an issue in our area. They always fought with [adjacent area] and that's where the sports centre is, that's where the [gang] is. So I mean I couldn't let my kid go over there himself. (*Parents' focus group, Newhouse*)

> Although we've got the big sports centre and the swimming pool and that, but when they're walking from here to the swimming pool, like my boy is going from a different scheme so there's always [the danger of trouble], if you come from a different scheme, do you know what I mean? So they're always – you always get that, not matter where the weans go.
> (*Parent, individual interview, Newhouse*)

Just as a gang might be seen as controlling a leisure centre or the route to it, a more informal club could also be regarded as 'owned' by an insider group:

> It's more like *their* club than for the, you know, anybody new or anything like. So kids can feel intimidated going into a youth club, unfortunately, you know, if as I say a bad element takes over, that's it, you know, it's awful difficult. (*Parents' focus group, Greenparks*)

Facilities such as sports centres at least offered a degree of adult supervision to counter worries about gangs, but even then some parents had concerns about the laxity or poor role modelling of the adults there:

> Em, well the local community centre used to hold a whole lot of stuff on, now we've not got a community centre for the kids. The [sports] centre, that does a lot for the kids but they have – they went through a stage, I think he was walking and the staff themselves were sitting smoking hash ...

I took my kids over and it was like one incident, my daughter got jumped by four girls in another area and all they could do was – they locked my daughter in a room and had all these four lassies shouting and bawling – there was no control over it whatsoever. The man who worked in the project, one of the staff, his eyes were glazed out his head, he didn't have a clue what was happening – full of drugs, you know.
(*Parents' focus group, Newhouse*)

Other spaces such as parks, rather than being seen as resources, could also be regarded as places containing a high degree of risk. Table 3.5 highlights how the majority of parents in all four study areas saw their local park as definitely unsafe or were unsure about its safety.

This was the case equally for some young people who highlighted risks of using parks:

Girl: It [the local area] is not a good place to play. Broken bottles and that. Dangerous.
Interviewer: So is it quite dangerous?
Girl: Yes.
Interviewer: What, because of the glass bottles?
Girl: And because we have got a big broken bit in our back, and broken stuff and that.
Interviewer: So broken stuff out the back. And you've got a big dump. What do you mean?
Girl: No like there is big bit where people, there's drugs and all that. Yes. And at the bottom of this, there is a big loch over there where me and my friends found needles and that.
Interviewer: Needles?
Girl: There was ones with caps off them and stuff and one was lying away from me with stuff on them.
(*Group 8, 10-year-old girls and boys, Newhouse*)

Table 3.5 How safe is your local park?

	No park (%)	Safe (%)	Not sure (%)	Unsafe (%)
Newhouse	10.5	18.4	28.9	42.1
Greenparks	23.8	28.6	26.2	21.4
Foundry	1.7	15.5	31.0	51.7
Yardinch	–	13.0	17.4	69.6

Conclusion

Parents and young people had a detailed understanding of their local area. The differentiation of their neighbourhoods was based on understandings of the people and behaviours that took place within them more than physical qualities. Moreover risks were perceived to vary according to time of day or week. For young people this depended on whether or not the areas represented immediate threats of violence. Parents similarly assessed whether an individual part of their neighbourhood was likely to be populated by familiar and trusted adults and children or by those who might be aggressive. A young person's familiarity with potentially threatening peers could reduce some risks, but this could be an unsatisfactory solution for parents who feared that it would lead not only to protection from gang members, but joining in their activities. This shows that parents saw risk not only in terms of threats to physical safety, but also as related to engagement in lifestyles that would both cause immediate problems and affect their children's life chances.

4.   Money, work and family life

Introduction

In this chapter attention turns to the financial aspects of disadvantage, with a focus on how money shapes family life. The findings underline complex forms of social exclusion related to the provision of material 'extras' beyond subsistence items such as food and shelter. As strategies for keeping children safe in relation to risks external to the home increasingly become paramount, the need to provide financially for organised activities outside the home may become a way in which risk is differentiated by income.

The majority of parents appeared to be coping adequately in terms of providing the material fundamentals (clothing, food and housing). Some, especially in the New Town area of Greenparks, had cars and apparently comfortable homes with digital televisions, game consoles and computers. There were a small number of striking exceptions, but it may be surmised that families in most extreme hardship declined to take part in the study. Some parents struggled to keep up with providing items that might be considered extras, such as fashionable brand-name clothes for their children. However, the interviews and discussion also revealed that there are powerful pressures in contemporary consumer-oriented society for these to be seen as essentials.

Parents felt under financial pressure to provide items that were hard to afford, but if their children lacked them it could result in bullying or peer-group exclusion. A parent in Newhouse explained: 'In secondary schools they pick on the ones with the Dunlop trainies.' Many parents saw their children's hobbies and out of school activities as part of their longer-term strategies for keeping their children 'on the right track', but these inevitably had cost implications.

The data collected pertaining to work and finances revealed a strong work ethic. Not only did many households feature two wage earners, but the importance of regular work was stressed by many parents when discussing their own roles or hopes for their children.

Figures 4.1 and 4.2 demonstrate the commitment to work in the households that completed the questionnaires. The great majority of parents who completed the questionnaire were female. This would explain the high rates of those who gave no information on partner's income; in the case of single-parent households there was no other source of income and in single wage-earner households the partner's income may have already been given for the first figure.

Across the sample as a whole, the two largest groups of households either derived their income from the work of both parents (104, 46 per cent), or had no income from work (82, 36 per cent). Less than one-fifth (42, 18 per cent) relied on a single wage. Sources of income were different for families with two parents, compared with single-carer families. Whereas 82 per cent of the former had at least one parent in full-time employment, this applied to less than a quarter of those on their own.

Figure 4.1 Source of income of parent who completed questionnaire

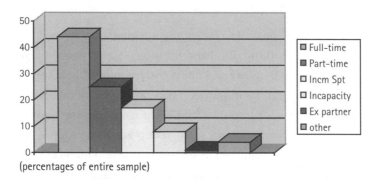

(percentages of entire sample)

Figure 4.2 Source of income of partner

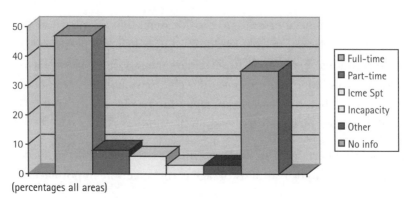

(percentages all areas)

Figure 4.3 Families claiming free school meals

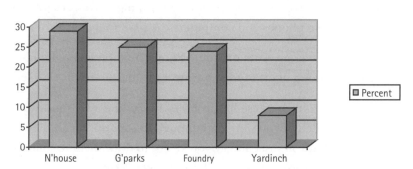

Correspondingly 43 per cent of lone parents derived their sole income from state benefits, but this was the case for only 11 per cent of parents with a partner.

Another indication of socio-economic disadvantage is registration for free school meals, although some who are eligible do not apply on account of stigma or other reasons. Of those who responded to the questionnaire, the proportion was at 23.5 per cent (Figure 4.3). Forty per cent of the single parents had children receiving free school meals. This suggests that despite having positive attitudes to work (see below), a large minority of families were still unable to provide the basics for their children.

Only 3 per cent of those in full-time work had children who received free school meals compared with 60 per cent of those whose income was derived from only part-time work or benefits. Car ownership was rare among those whose income was derived from part-time work or benefits. A higher proportion of single parents were in this group.

Managing on a limited income

In interviews parents described work as not only providing the means for basics and more expensive goods that form part of contemporary childhood but as also providing an important part of the culture of their family lives. In terms of providing basics and extra material goods, most parents felt pressure to keep up with modern lifestyles and technological innovations. Some felt extras like designer clothes and technological equipment were necessary for children to fit in with peers and at school. This added pressure and dictated in some ways the balance between work and family life.

> I don't think the difference is in dressing and feeding a wean, it's just that there is all the computer games and everything else ... . It's just the stress on the mobile phones and computers. (*Mother, Foundry*)

These extra costs exerting pressure on limited household budgets could have the knock-on effect of making items of everyday necessity harder to provide for:

> I feel really guilty because her trousers are getting a bit shot [worn]. You could be in debt if you were daft enough to fork out on all the things they could get, but you just cannae, you've got to draw the line somewhere, you know the pressure is definitely there. (*Mother, Foundry*)

This mother went on to say that she felt guilty when spending money on herself. Although parents often claimed that they were able to resist the pressure to spend too much money on material goods for their children, many clearly felt that buying such goods was part of the role of the contemporary parent. The following mother describes how she was finding provision of these extras difficult on one income.

> More financially nowadays because they want everything, you know, they want to keep up with their friends and that and most of their friends have two parents working. I worked and Brian worked, but now we're not together, it's a lot more of a struggle, you know to get them the things that you want to get them, but you cannae say aye to everything, you've got to say no at some point. (*Mother, Newhouse*)

Parents also wanted their children to take part in organised activities, which not only provided amusement for their children but also potentially developed social and practical skills:

> If you want your kids go dancing or swimming, you've got to be able to provide them with that wee extra bit of cash. (*Mother, Newhouse*)

Some families with one income or two parents with limited incomes thought they could only afford items and activities by getting into debt, especially around Christmas with its contemporary emphasis on consumerism. Some parents spoke of avoiding debts at all costs, whereas others talked of managing debt and some acknowledged difficulties in doing so. Attitudes towards other people getting into debt were sympathetic, because this was seen as an inevitable consequence of the increased material emphasis in contemporary childhoods and family lives. One mother said she got into debt so her daughter could keep up with the latest fashions being worn by her friends. Those parents who were on the most limited of incomes had to be inventive when providing for their children. One mother said she was able to provide a computer for her daughter's Christmas present by asking her to wait until after the holidays when they were able to buy one taken to a Cash Generator (a modern form of a pawn shop). Although her daughter was able to get her desired present, waiting until after Christmas to receive it may be seen as one form of social exclusion for children from poorer households. This parent also revealed other acts of creativity to manage on a low income such as scouring the adverts in the local paper for second-hand goods and rotating the giving of mobile phone credit to her three children. Another parent described the efforts she made to meet her children's needs, by use of low-cost sources of clothes and resisting pressures to buy electronic entertainments:

> I'm a bargain hunter. I go to Asda for their children's clothes ... I go round second-hand shops. I also have my Provident cheques that I can go to British Home Stores with, but I can pay that up pennies a week. I'm so terrified of debt, I even budget my debt ... I just budget constantly, catalogues are within my control. I mean it's not easy for a lot of folk they end up giving into their weans, my weans have never ha' a Sega or a computer game or anything. If I've no' got it, they don't get it and I don't go into debt for it. (*Mother, Yardinch*)

For other parents on limited incomes, letting young people know how much a family budget could sustain could be incorporated into an authoritative parenting pattern that moderated requests through explaining limits on expectations for young people:

> I'm very careful with money, I'm not one of these people that go out and just spend. I know I've got to keep me and the two girls, I've got to pay my bills. So I'll say to them, we've got this much, so if I take that out, we've still got enough to pay all the bills and feed us. (*Mother, Yardinch*)

Another way parents felt they could assist the management of a limited budget was through school uniforms. In a Yardinch discussion group all the parents present thought it was a good idea for children to wear uniforms, especially as the local supermarket sold the uniforms cheaply. The advantage was twofold in preventing comparison and stigmatisation of those with cheaper brands and also preserving children's out-of-school clothes.

Although parents were often able to provide the more expensive material extras, this often required careful organisation and long-term planning. Christmas provided a useful reference point to gain insight into how parents on limited incomes managed an event that could exert tremendous pressure on resources:

> Christmas, I started budgeting around about July. If I can't buy something
> with cash, I don't buy it, we'll go without for months and months. We want
> a new TV and I can't afford one just now. So we'll go without for a few
> months. There's no way I'll go into debt for a new TV. Make do with the
> one we've got until such a time we can afford one. So they know that they
> have to go without chocolate biscuits and all the wee treats.
> (*Mother, Greenparks*)

As previous research (Middleton and others 1995) has shown, financial contributions
directly to the children by relatives, normally grandparents, could alleviate pressures
on parents and extend the opportunities for the young people. The financial
transfers took varied forms, such as giving young people pocket money instead of
their parents, providing holidays and giving money for one off extra items that fell
outside of parents' day-to-day budgets.

Teaching young people about money

As well as providing the means for material goods, work was a means of promoting
certain values that parents found important, as the next quote shows:

> I'm a good parent, but my sister she isn't. She lets her son sit in the house,
> I mean he's 17 now, he's done nothing since he's left school ... she is going
> out working and she's giving him 35 pounds a week ... it's your self-respect,
> your self-worth and all getting out and getting a job isn't it? It's not just
> money. (*Mother, Newhouse*)

Parents often believed it set a good example to be seen to be working, especially if
young people could connect their parents working with the material things they
received. Helping young people understand the cost of things and have a notion of
budgeting was seen as vital to moderating requests for items and activities. One way
in which the relationship between money and application or conformity to desired
behavioural standards was encouraged in young people by parents was through
providing or withholding material rewards. Clothes, computer games or trips out
could be given for good behaviour or a certain standard of schoolwork. In one
example, two parents told how when a school trip to France was cancelled, they gave
their son the money set aside for the trip to spend on clothes and trainers. They
considered this to only be fair as their son had been promised the school trip as a
reward for his good behaviour and they felt that to be let down by the cancellation
would have sent a contradictory message. In another family a non-resident father

refused to give his son anything for Christmas because of his increasing non-attendance at school. However, the resident mother followed an opposite course of action, spending more than she could afford on her son's Christmas presents (a computer and scanner) in an attempt to get him going to school more consistently. Attitudes towards the relationship between money and reward were therefore not always consistent between or within families.

Exclusion from activities

Parents were often conscious that shortage of money limited their capacity to invest in activities to foster both current interests and future human capital for their children. This caused stress to parents and might result in the children being left out:

> Not a week goes by when she doesn't come home with a letter asking for money for a trip or some other. It just seems to be constantly money, money, money. I appreciate that they've got to raise funds and things but I feel they go on too many trips and I don't see the point of going on so many of them ... if I can't pay the money they get left behind in the classroom. (*Mother, Greenparks*)

One mother in Greenparks who had five children and no access to a car said she found it impossible to do things such as take her children swimming or to the ice-rink. Another mother felt her finances limited the number of dancing competitions her daughter could enter. These competitions included an entry fee for all members of the family who wanted to go, transport and a lunch each. Other parents complained about the cumulative cost of activities young people wanted to do with friends, which can present difficulties for people on fixed incomes.

> They're fed up because there's nothing for them to do. If they do go out, it costs money. You've got the sports centre or the fun pool ... it's all right people saying 'it's only a fiver or a tenner', it's a lot of money if you don't work. (*Mother, Foundry*)

By contrast, some parents saw having limited access to financial resources as enhancing young people's resilience, denying them the opportunity to do things detrimental to their health or life chances:

> I think because we've been on our own and he's seen me down and scrimping and saving, he's never had money for a drink or maybe a packet

of cigarettes. If I've not got it, he can't have it. When they used to hang around the chip shop and he didn't have money for chips it was hard for him, but now they've moved on to other things and he's never had the money for any of that. (*Mother, Yardinch*)

Another mother in the same community believed that her son's progress in his football career was partly as a consequence of their lack of money for other activities; he had instead chosen to 'kick a ball around'.

Organising work and family life

The necessity of work in the households studied, quite often with all available adults employed in some manner outside the home, caused difficulty in balancing the perceived demands of employment and parenting role. Many households were or had been dependent upon the help of extended family to allow a parent to work. Grandparents, even great-grandparents, would often look after children when parents' shifts did not coincide with school hours. Brothers and sisters of a parent could also fulfil this role, especially if they were parents themselves. In this respect extended family performed an important caring task that often depended on the reciprocity of all parties to keep it going. Links with kin often facilitated access to work, too.

Sometimes the necessity of work would impact negatively on family life within the household. Some parents complained of shift patterns playing havoc with family routines. In the following case a parent believed the deterioration in her son's behaviour was linked to her working and the upsetting of routines, with the child having to spend increasing amounts of his time at his grandmother's house.

> I'd rather have work that meant I was able to put him out to school and to be there when he comes home. Because I'm at work I'm finishing at half past seven at night. If I do get to see him before he goes to school, I don't see him until ten o'clock at night ... he's not getting his dinner at a set time because he'll not go down to my mum's when he comes in from school, he'll just go out with his pals and it's all upsetting. (*Mother, Newhouse*)

For this parent, as with many others, there was a palpable sense of guilt about her need to work and she felt constrained by the fact that only family-unfriendly working hours were available to her. She also pointed out how the money that her job provided gave them compensatory family time when out shopping:

> Like the only time we go out is maybe if we go shopping for clothes or things because he doesn't want to go to the pictures with me, he's got too old, he only wants to go out with his pals. (*Mother, Newhouse*)

In a household with two wage earners, a similar tension was felt between working and being able to provide opportunities for family treats:

> I suppose the kids have to understand that there's a trade off, we have to work so they can afford holidays and things and they know that. Their mum and dad have to work whereas a lot of their friends' parents don't, but they are aware of where money comes from, that it doesn't just come out of nowhere. If they want to have and do these things, mum and dad both have to work. (*Mother, Greenparks*)

Conclusions

The evidence showed that parents were on the whole successfully negotiating consumer pressures that are an integral part of contemporary parenting. However it would be complacent to see this as a sign of relative equality in society, for several reasons. A high proportion of households were receiving free school meals, indicating a reliance on this mean-tested assistance to provide the basics of subsistence. Even then, the stress of managing competing demands with a limited income was keenly felt. Probably families who declined to take part in the research included some who struggled even more.

To maximise incomes many parents were either engaged in full-time work or undertook shift work, which did not necessarily combine well with family life, having knock-on effects for stress and management of time. These income and work considerations interacted with parental fears about their children being ostracised for failing to meet peer expectations and the risks associated with undirected activity for young people in their communities. The latter could be addressed by participation in hobbies and organised activity for young people with appropriate supervision, but the cost and organisational implications of that can impact greatly on stretched household budgets. This is a key process by which positive parenting strategies can made more difficult in such environments, as we shall see in the next chapter.

5. Keeping young people safe and the role of discipline

Given the significant risks identified in the preceding chapters it is important to look at the strategies employed by parents to keep children safe (this chapter) and those used by children themselves (next chapter). Both parties took account of each other's viewpoints and, in part, strategies developed interactively. Open communication between parents and children was a prominent feature in their accounts of how parents sought to influence or control their children's behaviour. This applied both to the approach to discipline described by many of them and also the ways in which they helped their children manage external risks and keep safe. Parents adapted their disciplinary and risk management strategies to their children's ages and personalities. They were also based on the understanding of how particular places could be safe or risky for children at different times, as identified in Chapter 3 of this report.

Influencing and controlling young people's play and leisure time

Most parents believed they could influence how young people spent their time outside the home. Forty-three per cent in the questionnaire survey believed they could influence this a lot and 52 per cent to some extent (Table 5.1). Sixty per cent of parents said that their children always had to ask for permission to go out and 33 per cent claimed this happened 'most times or sometimes'. Only 5 per cent said their children never asked permission to go out. Perhaps most telling was the high percentage of parents claiming to give their children a definite time to be home (88 per cent 'always', 10 per cent 'sometimes').

This high level of claimed knowledge fitted with what parents said in interviews. Knowing where their children were was part of their discourse of the 'good' parent. Tracking children's whereabouts was a multi-purpose task to not only assess the safety

Table 5.1 Influencing children outside the home

	Always (%)	Sometimes (%)	Never (%)
Do you require your child to ask permission to go out?	136 (60%)	75 (33%)	12 (5%)
Do you ask your child where they are going?	211 (91%)	15 (5%)	–
Do you give a certain time to be back?	203 (88%)	21 (10%)	1 (4%)

of their own children but also check whether their children were presenting a risk or nuisance to others in the community. Especially with older children, fears were as much about them getting into trouble through their behaviour as about direct harm. Thus, at times parental worries about safety shaded into concern about longer-term risk shaping the life chances of young people. They wanted their children to avoid negative lifestyles associated with crime, alcohol, drugs, anti-school culture and so on.

The strategies went further than simply asking children to be in at a certain time or them having to ask permission to go out. Most parents sought to manage actively the balance of risk and safety connected to how young people spent their leisure time. Five principal strategies were identified in the qualitative data: *the removal of risks; monitoring; communication; rules and discipline; directed associations and the use of trusted network members.* Other research has shown monitoring and supervision to be key components of how 'ordinary' parents conceive their caring, guidance and protective roles (Stace and Roker 2004). The various strategies often operated alongside one another. There was a rough correspondence between type of strategy and the child's age (Table 5.2). Removal of risks and direct monitoring strategies were more

Table 5.2 Summary of appropriateness of parental safety strategies to child age and perceived proximity of risk

Parental strategy	Child age stage	Proximity of risk to the household
Removal of risks	Early childhood	Close to home
Monitoring	Early childhood	Close to home
Communication, rules and discipline	Mid to late childhood	In wider community
Directed association	Mid to late childhood	In wider community
Trusted network members	Mid to late childhood	In wider community

commonly used for younger children as these required direct action by the parent and were more feasible when the child and the perceived risks were in close proximity to the household.

In the remainder of this section, the first three strategies will be explored. The other two, with their emphasis on community and network resources, feature in Chapter 7 on networks, support and social capital.

Removal of risks

A small number of parents referred to direct action aimed at tackling a particular risk. A few reacted so badly to their neighbourhood that they wanted to leave altogether. For poor families this option was restricted to requesting a move to their social landlord. A number had asked to be re-housed, usually on account of problem neighbours but this was usually a lengthy process, requiring great investments of time and effort.

On a smaller scale, some parents sought to remove threats from their micro-environment, such as picking up used needles before allowing a child to play on grass. A number of children of different ages said their parents locked the house when they were in, presumably as a means of excluding dangerous intruders.

Parental monitoring

All the parents interviewed claimed to know where their children were all of the time. The way in which they sought to keep abreast of their children's whereabouts and activities altered as children grew older and wanted to spend more time away from home. The *direct supervision* approach was more appropriate for younger children and overlaps at this age with the removal of risks since it can entail confining a child to places seen as devoid of dangers, such as the home. Consequently, keeping younger children at home or close to home with a family member was an important element in managing the play of younger children, so they were not exposed to the threats seen to exist beyond the immediate vicinity of home outlined in Chapter 3. *Visual monitoring* entered parental strategies for early excursions of children away from the direct supervision of parents. Allowing children to play outside the home, parents described ensuring children stayed close enough that they could still be seen or heard from the house. This would also be accompanied by the setting of *physical boundaries* for children to play in the garden or part of the street near their home. Younger children were also expected to be within calling distance at all times. For these children the spaces they occupied were therefore made safe by the high levels of parental supervision and close boundary settings:

> Michael might go out the front and play but he's still only eight – he's only out until roughly maybe about eight o'clock and he's in. But I don't, I really don't like them going out and hanging about. If anything, I don't mind you going out in the back garden, that's fine, I'd rather you were out there than actually out there, that's my own – but he'll go out there and he'll play with his pals and go to their gardens and bits and pieces, or go up to the square bit. (*Mother, Greenparks*)

Children of all ages mentioned that they were not allowed to visit areas viewed by their parents as 'unsafe'. They mainly related this to parents' concerns about potential threats from other *adults*: strange people, drug addicts, alcoholics and paedophiles in the local area, as well as gangs of young people in three of the four areas.

When children moved further afield, especially as they grew older, direct personal supervision became impractical. Strategies thus shifted to intermittent contact and *distance checks* such as expecting young people to return to base periodically. Some young people, such as the 12- and 14-year-olds below, understood why their parents required checking back, but also described how it interfered with their play and autonomy:

> *Boy*: It's annoying because even if you're playing a game it's hard to get a good game in an hour and a half.
> *Girl*: Aye cause they aw get a game and then when ye want to be two hours jist to get a big game wae aw. That's roon the scheme an' that.
> *Interviewer*: So every hour and a half you have to come in?
> *Girl*: Aye.
> (*12-year-old girl and 14-year-old boy, Foundry*)

Children's use of mobile phones made it much easier for distance checks to be made on a child's whereabouts or well-being. Young people from 10 to 14 years old mentioned that they were asked to take mobile phones when going out and that parents regularly called them to check they were all right. Certain children said their parents phoned them every half hour. Children also reported that parents made sure their child's phone had credit. Most parents also occasionally employed an *accompanying* strategy particularly in regard to evening or night-time journeys. Those with cars preferred to give children a lift. However, many of the interviewees who did not own a car maintained a monitoring strategy through a detailed knowledge of bus timetables and the approximate time taken for children to walk from A to B. In areas where it was considered there was a high risk of being hassled by gangs, parents would meet their children off a bus.

Communication, rules and discipline

When children moved beyond their parents' direct or indirect purview, then they had to rely on their children's understandings of expectations and rules, and their commitment to them. This in turn depended on communication about what was expected. It was in relation to this strategy that the perception of risks began to shape internal processes within the home most profoundly. When children became more independent and parental monitoring was no longer seen as appropriate, rules about boundaries, expected standards of behaviour and times to be home became a proxy for parental monitoring and direct supervision. Strikingly parents and young people alike recognised that rules and sanctions were essential, but could only work well if underpinned by discussion and explanation. The most commonly described discipline process involved discussion, reinforced by grounding or the denial of treats of privileges, following a rule transgression. Both generations stressed the importance of negotiation and democratic family decision-making about what children could or could not do, though this was qualified by parents' ultimate authority, young people's strategies to withhold information and the use of punishments for the transgression of agreed standards and expectations. Given parents' universal fears about the effects of local risks on their children's immediate safety and long-term life chances, these communication-based strategies were adopted not simply for idealised reasons about the best way to be a parent but on pragmatic grounds in that they were seen as working effectively.

Parents monitored young people's associations outside the home and directed activities, but it was recognised that no matter how much monitoring parents employed they could not, in the words of one mother, 'choose their pals for them'. In the face of risks, some parents saw the best response as being to help young people develop an 'orientation to risk' that enabled them to draw the most from their peer groups but also to be resilient to attendant risks. This involved developing a sense of risk awareness, learning when a situation could potentially turn into trouble, or being aware of the effects of drugs and alcohol. The risks at large in disadvantaged communities were seen by some parents as opportunities for handling risk from an early age:

> My son, he sees it. He goes on the streets at night, hangs about with his friends at night and sees the junkies and whatever. I call them drug addicts, he calls them black bobs and mankies whatever ... you're just instilling in them – you just don't go there, there's better things to do, you can choose a better life. (*Mother, Newhouse*)

Below a parent shows how perceived risks in her community could be pre-empted by discussion:

> You just have to keep discussing it with them and if there's an opportunity, if something's on the television and they ask a question be prepared to answer it as honestly as you can. I have discussed drugs with them and they have – I mean I don't think I've anything to worry about in that score, I don't think they'd ever do that but you can never say never, can you? I mean they go on at me for smoking – they're always on at me for smoking so I think I know what, how they feel about things like that. But I do try and discuss it with them. If they ask a question, I'll try and answer it honestly. And I think they feel comfortable enough with me to ask me anything. The same with their dad, I think they can ask their dad anything. (*Parent interview, Newhouse*)

Responding to the infringement of rules

In the questionnaires several possible responses to the transgression of rules were put to parents (Figure 5.1). Interestingly, grounding was the mechanism used often by more people (about a third), though this was closely followed by discussion, which

Figure 5.1 How often parents use the following discipline responses

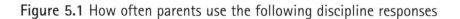
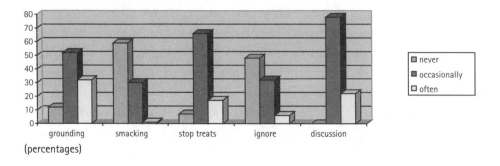

(percentages)

Figure 5.2 Parental ratings of responses to bad behaviour

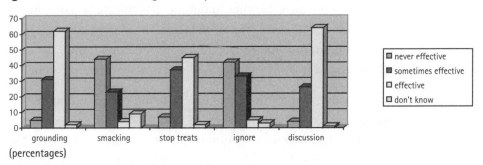

(percentages)

was thus a common means of reacting to as well as seeking to prevent risky behaviour. However, large numbers of people said they used discussion occasionally and nobody reported never using this strategy, while 10 per cent said they never grounded their children. Stopping treats was the next most common practice. Ignoring the child was an approach adopted by over half of parents, for the most part only now and then. Smacking was hardly ever admitted to as a frequent practice, but nearly one-third of the parents said they smacked occasionally (usually claiming in the qualitative data that this was something they did when children were younger).

Asked about the effectiveness of these five discipline strategies, nearly two-thirds thought both discussion and grounding were invariably effective and most others said they were sometimes. Most also regarded stopping treats as effective at least some of the time. By contrast over 40 per cent stated that smacking and ignoring were never effective:

The frequency of reference to grounding did not necessarily mean it was the most used strategy, however. Closer examination of the accounts of grounding revealed it to be the culmination of other more circumspect and pre-emptive discipline styles, involving various forms of warning, explanation and discussion. In this regard, grounding and the allied response of stopping treats were a last resort disciplinary response when more everyday processes of discussing expectations and boundaries had failed. Other reactive responses such as shouting at children or smacking were referred to, but adults by and large saw these as unconstructive and unreflective responses to bad behaviour. In the example of the following mother, physical punishment is seen as inferior to discussion:

> One time I gave her a smack and I done it as a relief and I'm saying – 'Well, that's wrong!' I could have sat and spoke to her instead of doing that.
> (*Mother, Yardinch*)

The majority of parents disapproved of physical punishments or saw it as a personal failing, but a minority spoke disapprovingly of society's censorial attitude towards physical punishment as the removal of a parental right in favour of a children's right. A small number of parents revealed that they found the new culture of parenting something they found difficult to enact. This would suggest not every parent accepted the liberal consensus on child-rearing practices. Although it was not exclusively men who reported it, their expression of this view was more common:

> They say smacking's bad for them and this, that and the next thing. When I was young I was scared of the teachers so I wouldn't do it, you know, it was a deterrent. And now there's nothing. The kids say, 'So, I can do what I want, you cannae touch me! I'll 'phone this and I'll 'phone that ...' You shouldn't have to argue with kids. They should sit and listen to what you're saying. (*Father, Newhouse*)

> I think they've really got to have rules, personally, I think they've got to have rules ... when I was at school you were frightened of like the police, when the police would appear. But nowadays they've got so many rights and they're – you can see, you can see their point of view and say – Yes, okay you've got to have rules so that you don't hurt the children but then you've got to have other sort of rules so that they know how far they can go. (*Father, Greenparks*)

Children's views on rules and punishments

The questionnaire responses by children highlighted their autonomy within the constraints of established rules for reporting their whereabouts and activities to parents. Table 5.3 reveals that telling parents of their whereabouts, who they are with and what time they will be in were common practices in households. It does however contradict parents' typical *belief* that they knew of their children's whereabouts. Young people reported that parents did not always know their whereabouts and, strikingly, 47 per cent reported their parents never knew *what* they were doing even if they knew where they were. The explanation for this discrepancy can be found in how young people use discussion and parental openness to maintain a space and identity away from parental control, a device that has been reported elsewhere (Solomon and others 2002).

The young people's questionnaire data did however support, if a little less convincingly, parental reports of discipline strategies. Both explanation and discussion were reported to be the most common responses to wrongdoing. The children reaffirmed that smacking was an out-of-favour discipline response, but

Table 5.3 Children's response to question about parent/guardian's rules: do you have to do any of the following?

Parental rules	Always (%)	Sometimes (%)	Never (%)
Ask permission to go out	59 (23%)	107 (41%)	83 (32%)
Tell them where you are going	107 (41%)	114 (44%)	30 (12%)
Tell them who you will be with	74 (29%)	107 (41%)	67 (26%)
Say when you will be in	124 (48%)	97 (37%)	29 (11%)
Say what you will be doing	30 (12%)	96 (37%)	122 (47%)

Table 5.4 What do your parents/guardians do if you do something they think is wrong?

Parent action if something wrong N (%)	Always (%)	Sometimes (%)	Never (%)
Do nothing	9 (3%)	67 (26%)	144 (56%)
Stop pocket money/treats	21 (8%)	76 (29%)	128 (49%)
Ground me	61 (24%)	110 (42%)	65 (25%)
Smack me	10 (4%)	14 (5%)	205 (79%)
Shout at me	74 (29%)	143 (55%)	25 (9%)
Explain why it's wrong	104 (40%)	92 (33%)	42 (16%)
Discuss what I have done	84 (32%)	97 (37%)	53 (20%)

29 per cent claimed they were 'always' shouted at and 55 per cent 'sometimes'. Three-quarters of children said they were grounded at least sometimes.

However, despite these discrepancies between young people's and parent's accounts of discipline, the interviews revealed broadly similar accounts of household processes concerning rules and expectations. Many parental expectations identified by young people focused around keeping them out of trouble or avoiding behaviours deleterious to themselves or the neighbourhood, as much as their own safety. These rules could be about who young people were not allowed to play with (those seen as posing a risk) or quite specific rules about what activities were forbidden, such as fighting, coming home drunk or being brought home by the police.

> Well my mum won't let me hang about with boys or other people that talk about drugs and that ... I mean, I don't want to hang around with people like that. (*12-year-old boy, Greenparks*)

> Aye, she has no objection to me going out as long as I don't come home in the back of a police car and I don't come home pure steaming.
> (*14-year-old boy, Foundry*)

When shouting or being smacked was referred to, children mirrored the parental belief that it did little to resolve discipline problems. In the words of one 14-year-old boy from Foundry: 'It doesn't get through, it's in one ear and out the other.'

Children and young people reported that grounding was a common feature of parental discipline. It usually followed the infringement of a well-established rule or expectation, acknowledging that grounding could follow 'a tellin' or discussion. Often a grounding and explanation would be used together to underline the severity of the infringement (something that the questionnaire would not detect). It was evident that young people understood there to be a behavioural contract whereby they would be grounded if they broke established rules. Young people were able to give reasons for the occasions they had been grounded and indicate it was a just response:

> Aye, I think it is fair because if I'm given a certain time to be in and I'm no' then that's me breaking a rule. (*Boy, aged 14, Newhouse*)

Young people described how parental expectations focused around safety, household management and preventing conflict between siblings. Household management would correspond to tasks around the home parents expected young people to do. However, the vast majority of rules or expectations young people reported were linked to safety when outside the home. This included rules about times to be in, being where they said and keeping away from certain places. Thus rules were used to manage the place, person, time and activity combinations highlighted as risky in Chapter 3.

An important finding was the high degree to which young people felt cared for by parents making and enforcing rules. Children valued the support of parents in recognising the risky nature of play and leisure time. Inevitably however, rules could also be seen as constraining. They often created tensions between desires to stay out with friends and abide by parents' wishes. Some young people reported strategies to divert or subvert parental monitoring, such as forgetting their watch or mobile phones, switching off the mobile or resetting the time when they came home. However, there was also evidence of rules being negotiated so that young people could stay out later at certain times such as weekends and school holidays. Yet it was those very times when young people had most free time and sought freedom to use it, that some areas posed the most risk. Rules often were in place to reflect this tension.

The importance of a consistent message

A feature of parents' discussion of standards and expectations in relation to risk was the necessity for a consistent message to be given over an extended period of time.

> Too many, I think, give in too easily, I honestly think people give in too –
> maybe I'm hard, but that is my honest opinion because they'll think long
> and hard before they do anything to make you make that threat, because
> it's not worth it because once you've made that threat you're going to see
> that right through. I think that's a lot of people go wrong there, I've heard
> them saying – 'That's it, you're not getting this and you're not getting that,'
> and then you turn round and they're giving them pounds.
> (*Parent, Yardinch*)

The above quote illustrates the perceived importance of maintaining a consistent message and not 'giving in' to young people. Grounding or denying privileges requires further consistency as unlike smacking or shouting, grounding required supervision by parents that could restrict their own activities and relaxation. Hence it became tempting to relent. Children recognised that parents could find grounding difficult to apply, which presented them with an opportunity to modify its application. Some reported being let out prior to the agreed time limit and even engineering situations in which to make this more likely:

> I get grounded and then I get let out: fifteen minutes and I've worked my
> way out of the house, I just talk when she is trying to watch Eastenders or
> something like that and then she will just let me out.
> (*Children's group interview, Foundry*)

A similar way in which children could undermine parental consistency is by playing parents off one another, which was even easier to achieve when parents did not share a residence.

Interaction between children and parents

Traditionally, research on discipline styles has been based on a parent-centric model of the relationship between discipline style and child outcomes (for example, Baumrind 1978). It suggested that a parent chooses a style freely without constraint from circumstances or the children's individual characteristics. Recent work has recognised that issues of control in families is more situation-specific and in some ways negotiated. The children's comments above on grounding and consistency showed how they could influence the follow-through of threatened or actual punishments. In this study parents talked about discipline in a way that revealed they believed there was an interaction between child characteristics and their discipline style. This is another contributing factor to add alongside the environmental factors discussed previously.

Several observed that some children were easier than others so punishment was rarely required:

> Fortunately my kids are quite good, you know. But I have seen a lot of kids who have really pushed their parents, you know. Take their stuff off them, that's it. (*Mother, Newhouse*)

> I don't really have bad behaviour ... I can't say they've done anything in life that's been that bad ... Steven very rarely goes out, he never has done. (*Mother, Newhouse*)

In this last example the son's insularity caused concern, but also shaped the mother's discipline response, meaning that groundings were not as necessary, nor would they have been appropriate. It is noteworthy that it is the child's characteristics that are accredited with producing the behaviour rather than success as a parent and decisions about discipline. Not uncommonly though, other parents were criticised for allowing certain behaviour:

> You know, we don't have the bad language, we don't have the bad mouthing back to us. Yeah, on occasions you do but not to any of the extreme that you get, that we have heard from family and friends' children, that we wouldn't tolerate. (*Mother, Greenparks*)

In other instances parents cited the characteristics of their child as shaping their discipline strategy. The quote below shows how the strategy of ignoring a child was regarded as effective with a child particularly sensitive to loss of maternal attention:

> There was something he had done that had really had it and I thought, 'I'm not going to shout, I'm not going to scream,' and I thought 'I'm just totally ignoring him ...' He was like, 'You're not talking to me,' and I let it go all day and it was the next day, he was like 'Are you talking to me yet?' and I said 'I don't know, are you a nicer person than you were yesterday?' It worked, it worked a treat it really did. (*Mother, Greenparks*)

Parents also adapted their approach to differences between siblings as in the case of Martin and Amy below. Here, the son was seen as having a set of problems that made him difficult to parent whilst his sister was seen as offering no problems at all:

Well I've had problems with Martin, especially. Martin – he's quite paranoid, he thinks people talk about him all the time. I used to jump to his defence all the time until I got wise to it and realised that it wasn't always the other person, sometimes it was him that was in the wrong, and that's quite difficult. I found that difficult because if you tell him he's in the wrong then he accuses me of not being a good parent, you know, of hating him – oh! Amy, I can't actually say much about Amy because she's never given me any problems, she's always been quite easy. (*Mother, Greenparks*)

The next example shows both sibling difference and how a child could lead a parent to question whether grounding is ineffective. If a child coped well with being confined to the house, grounding could be welcomed or treated with (apparent) indifference rather than experienced as a punishment, which one mother thought might be gender related.

Steven's more kind of like, oh, he doesn't really care that much. You know, see if you say: 'Well do you know what, you're not going outside that door for two days!' ... 'Okay then,' and just plonks away up the stairs, you know. He just doesn't care. I don't know if it's a boy thing but he just doesn't.

The same mother reported further challenges to the punishment:

He'll pop downstairs and go in and make himself a cup of tea and say 'Hiya!' and I thought 'He's really trying to annoy me!' Do you know what I mean? Where I'm trying to annoy him by keeping him in, I think he tries to annoy me by constantly traipsing out and in and out and in and out and in, giving me a big smile as if to say – 'But you've not annoyed me!' So it's a sort of a battle of wills, really.

Yet the strategy seemed to work with his sister:

If you snib Kirsty when she's done wrong, Kirsty goes into her room and only comes out when necessary because she knows – where he doesn't care.

Conclusions: Discipline style and resilience in high-risk communities

Discipline was revealed to be part of a wider process of ongoing communication in households, which in turn was connected to the risks young people faced. In recent years, family relationships have come to be interpreted within the idea of the pure relationship as becoming ever more democratic (Giddens 1992). It is not a true democracy, however; parents have the balance of power on their side, while young people can manipulate situations to their own advantage (such as through managing the information they give to their parents) (Solomon and others 2002). Nevertheless, a high value was placed on discussion and negotiation in households by parents who are, to a greater degree than young people, establishing the rules of households.

In terms of the wider questions of this report we need to ask how these processes intersect with the contexts of the higher risk communities the families reside in. In one important way the discipline responses correspond neatly with evidence presented in the section on perceptions of area, notably that not only are certain sub-areas in the community seen as risky, but more crucially it was precise combinations of places, people, times and activities that made for greater risks. In such a situation, strategies for keeping young people safe need to become complex so that young people can both harness developmental benefits within their community (friendship, activity, independence) and avoid the risks (dangers to self, becoming dangers to others and those affecting their long-term life chances). Both formal and informal spaces may offer opportunities but also embody risks, often depending on who would be there at different times, so inflexible sets of parent-issued instructions about places may not best serve the best interests of parents or young people. Additionally, young people become the experts in certain fields such as the peer group, sites of informal leisure and school, often knowing the balance of risk and safety more clearly than parents themselves.

The discipline styles that were disregarded as ineffective by parents were those that undermined a relationship in which discussion and communication could flourish. Those styles that were seen as ideal involved a rational discourse between parent and young person, though both parties reported examples of more indirect or non-verbal bargaining. Grounding was also significant because, after events when understandings about risk and safety had not been shared by adults and young people, it removed young people from the risky spaces until such a time that the understanding had been re-established. Some young people, though, sought to undermine grounding through indifference or subversive reaction.

6. Children's accounts of the negotiation of safety and risk in their communities

Introduction

The methods children described for keeping themselves safe and minimising threats were characterised by resilience processes operating at the individual and collective level. Although often undertaken with the support and facilitation of parents, the children's interviews revealed that they were often active agents in ensuring their own safety, applying their own knowledge of the local community or relying on each other.

Negotiating place, person, time and activity

In Chapter 3 it was noted that young people in each study area identified certain places as unsafe. Sometimes young people would talk about characteristics of the physical environment (notably the presence of litter or graffiti) that marked them out as unsafe. However, closer discussion revealed it was usually the behaviours that occurred in areas that gave them their sense of danger, though this might be signified by objects like broken glass and discarded needles. These were places where individuals were known to have been attacked or where local gangs, drug addicts, 'neds' or people drinking hung out. These locations were more likely to be seen as dangerous places if they were dark. Children had no control over the places themselves, but did adapt to their perceived characteristics. One strategy was to stay in familiar safe areas and avoid these danger spots, either altogether or at night. However young people said they could negotiate these same risky areas with relative safety, for example when going to them with friends or during the daytime. Thus children's local knowledge helped them develop safety approaches that complemented the threats with regard to timing and presence of trusted or feared people. In interviews, children reported accompanying one another home or using their mobile phones to check friends had reached home safely once they had parted.

Staying in safe areas and returning at unsafe times

Younger children described how they played only in their garden and street, while older participants described how they stayed in their own scheme or only visited other areas where they knew people. A significant number stated that they simply did not go out. Some of the young respondents voiced the same views as parents that keeping off the streets and taking part in directed activities was a key means of keeping safe. They spoke of keeping safe by going to youth or football clubs:

> *Interviewer*: Why is the youth club good for you?
> *Boy*: It keeps us away from fights, because if we were just hangin' about and someone started fighting us, we would be in here.
> (*Focus group, 12-year-old boys, Greenparks*)

> My fitba team keeps me aff the streets! (*14-year-old boy, Yardinch*)

When children ventured further during the day, the coming of darkness signalled a retreat to safe areas. Younger respondents talked about coming in when it was dark and the older ones how they came in at a 'decent time'.

Transport offered safe passage through risky places. Children of all ages told of how their parents would provide lifts or accompany them to places. Some older ones mentioned taking taxis or buses without supervision.

Avoidance of places and people

The corollary of staying in areas regarded as safe was to avoid certain places especially where potential aggressors were likely to be. Young people also identified specific individuals, groups of people and situations they would avoid. Younger children commented that they would avoid 'teenagers', whereas older respondents would specify that they avoided teenagers who had been drinking. There was other evidence of young people differentiating their peers as risky or safe in the language they used, talking of 'neds' and gang members as people of their own age group or older whom they contrasted with friends and avoided. Other individuals that respondents mentioned avoiding were known drug users whilst younger children also listed strangers.

Ten to 14-year-olds described how they would stay away from gangs or took an alternative route to avoid them. A few had even mentioned hiding (in bushes, for example) when seeing gangs. Another strategy given by older children was to make no eye contact when passing gangs in the street. More than one child reported staying off school to avoid people who they were having conflict with. This protected them from the current risk, but if persistent might jeopardise their longer-term life chances.

Staying clear of threatening persons was also applied to dealing with strangers. This was more an issue for younger respondents than older ones. They described occasions when they had been approached by adults they did not know and some described particular adults they were wary of. Eight and 10-year-olds in Newhouse Primary spoke of the 'run and tell' rule. While they reeled it off in a parrot-like fashion, they also described how, among other strategies, they could incorporate this into their repertoire of responses.

Managing peer relationships

Central to young people's accounts of keeping safe and noticeably absent from parents' perspectives was the importance of managing relationships with peers.

An important part of strategies for avoiding dangerous situations was for young people to make sure they were not alone. Both younger and older interviewees commented that they stayed with friends when playing outside, explaining that this way they were less likely to get bullied, hassled or attacked when in a group.

Respondents told how they would walk each other home at night or send text messages to make sure friends had reached destinations safely. In one extreme example a 12-year-old boy's parents had been attacked in their own home. The boy reported that in the following period he would allay his own safety fears by staying at a friend's or having friends stay over. It was apparent that even those as young as eight years old would go to help each other:

> There's people around the corner and they were getting bullied so I went over to them. At the time I didn't know them and I said 'What's wrong?' and they went 'People are bullying me,' and then she said they were calling her stuff like that wasn't nice ... I went back home and I told my mum and my mum took her back in the house and they discussed it. And I was sitting beside the girl asking her questions so I was making her feel better and make her cheer up. (*8-year-old, Yardinch*)

Older children would also look after younger children. This was reported by both older children, who gave examples of taking younger children to the park, and by younger children who had been taken places by the older ones.

However, the safety associated with this had to be weighed against the fact that being in a large group could make young people appear to be looking for trouble.

> *Interviewer*: What do you do to keep safe?
> *Girl 1*: Don't go into their place, I just hang round with a big gang.
> *Girl 2*: I don't hang about with a big gang, maybe one or two people because if you are in a gang, other people think you want trouble.
> (*Focus group, 13-year-old girls, Foundry*)

Parents also reported that large groups of young people could appear threatening and might lead to the police being called.

It was also suggested that children do not have to be with another person in order to be safe, and that simply being connected to another person was often enough. Some interviewees mentioned that because their older brothers or sisters were known they would not get drawn into trouble or bullied. Some children reported pretending to have an older brother or sister to older children, whereas others ingeniously pretended to be on their mobile phone when walking past people who gave them cause for concern.

Avoiding peer conflicts was another way that young people felt they could manage the risks that faced them. This could involve having a policy of 'keeping out of other people's business' and not getting involved when friends fell out. Some respondents indicated that they stayed safe by not drawing attention to themselves or doing anything that might provoke a reaction.

> I've learned to keep my head down because I'm quite a hyper person, laughing silly and being the little person at school, I would get made fun of doing that now. So, I've learned to keep my head down, I don't dress differently or anything like that. (*14-year-old girl, Greenparks*)

Another way of avoiding trouble was not to reveal loyalties to a particular football team at times when tensions between supporters could be incendiary (after an Auld Firm match between Celtic and Rangers, for example). After a controversial game between the two teams, young people reported not wearing their football strips out of doors. This strategy was backed up by parents who often reported encouraging support of a different team that incurred less fierce local rivalry. This however proved difficult given such teams were considered less fashionable, carrying less *cachet* in the peer group.

The role of parents and other adults

Young people in the study reaffirmed independently the role of parents and key adults in keeping them safe, as is also described in Chapters 5 and 7. Mobile phones were ubiquitous in the lives of young people, and their role in keeping young people safe was crucial. In Chapter 5 it was noted that parents kept their children safe by asking them where they were going, with whom and what time they were expected back, and with intermittent contact over the period of time in which they were out. Young people also mentioned such monitoring strategies when talking about how they kept safe, usually suggesting they felt partners in this process rather than being under surveillance. Respondents of all ages reported always telling a parent where they were going and younger children revealed it reassured them that someone would know if they were to go missing. Older children also welcomed intermittent contact, and felt safe knowing someone could come and collect them if there was a problem. Two sisters (aged 11 and 14) on an early visit into the city centre described how they asked their father to call regularly to check they were fine. Some older respondents did not welcome the contact when out, as it could be embarrassing or intrusive, but they recognised that it kept them safe.

Other adults were also mentioned as a resource for keeping young people safe, such as grandparents and, interestingly on account of them not featuring in parent's accounts, teachers and janitors, who were seen as maintaining their safety whilst at school. Various incidents were described in which a young person had been bullied at school, and some involved had informed a teacher. If the bullying took place outside school, there were reports of parents being told and of them approaching the parents of the person who bullied their children.

Coping alone

The converse of taking or seeking support to confront threatening areas, individuals or groups was a preference for dealing with a situation unaided, when it was considered that outside interference could make things worse. For example, while some children said teachers would assist safety with respect to peer aggression, others told how involving teachers could exacerbate bullying by causing an escalation of the issue. Also while older children sometimes offered protection to younger ones, some, of course, would be those who bullied. The combination of potential support and harm could be embodied in the same individual, as was particularly the case with older siblings who could be a source of both protection and bullying. Some young people expressed confusion over how to react to provocation, as they were aware of conflicting messages to either ignore those who bullied them, or stand up to them. The quotes below show that not only could following adult advice make problems worse, but children had learned from experience that ignoring or accepting attacks seemed a sensible strategy for avoiding further trouble:

> *Boy*: I just ignore them.
> *Interviewer*: Do you?
> *Boy*: My dad says to hit back because you don't let them get away with it.
> *Interviewer*: Do you hit back?
> *Boy*: Well, they didnae hit me a lot but after I hit one, they all came after me.
> (*8-year-old boy, Foundry*)

> *Interviewer*: Do you ever get hassled?
> *Girl*: Yeah, I've had a golf ball threw at me, I've been spat on hundreds.
> *Interviewer*: And what have you done when that happens?
> *Girl*: Tried to ignore it because to retaliate they would all jump on me.
> *Interviewer*: So what do you do when that has happened?
> *Girl*: If I've been spat on, I'll go home and get washed but nothing really, you just have to accept it.
> *Interviewer*: Do you talk to your friends?
> *Girl*: Yeah, go home and talk to my friends.
> *Interviewer*: Do you talk to your parents?
> *Girl*: Yeah, but I find it embarrassing sometimes, in case they think I can't take care of myself.
> (*14-year-old, Greenparks*)

Getting drawn in

Inevitably, not all individuals were able to maintain their own safety in the face of the risks they came into contact with. Sometimes, perhaps confused by competing advice to react to or ignore aggressive behaviour from others, or not simply being able to avoid it, young people became drawn into conflict.

> I was walking down and this boy had come down and he said he wanted to fight me and I said no, he then, he tripped me up and he just pulled a baseball bat out of his top and started swinging at me. He was from the

[names place]. They come up here and fight the Greenparks.
(*12-year-old boy, Greenparks*)

Conclusion: Young people's resilience in enabling them to keep safe

Although young people shared their parent's concerns and many of the strategies to keep themselves safe, it is also notable how adept young people were in developing their own strategies, both collectively in their friendship groups and alone. The findings here offer more support to the idea that 'directed activity' has both long-term and short-term safety consequences for young people. Perhaps understandably, young people were more likely to identify the short-term consequences of such activities, keeping them out of immediate danger, whereas their parents took the longer view.

However, the role of adults was not an unequivocally helpful one. Young people spoke of how seeking safety in numbers could mean adults in the community seeing them as a threat, and there was also ambiguity as to how to respond to bullying, exacerbated by conflicting messages from key adults. If young people are to be encouraged to report incidents of bullying, this data suggests that adults must be able to offer protection for those reporting.

7. Community, support and social capital

Introduction

In this chapter we look at how parents and young people navigate the networks within their communities to ensure short-term safety and enhance life chances.

Help and support from others

On the questionnaire parents were asked if they had people to whom they could turn for help and support in their role as parent. Over three-quarters of respondents (77 per cent) indicated that they did have people who helped in this way. Compared with the main sample, a slightly higher proportion of single parents said they had no one who helped (34 per cent to 23 per cent) as Ghate and Hazel (2002) found.

Family members, friends and neighbours were evidently the main sources of support. Respondents' estimates of the number of people who helped out ranged from one to 30, with over half the answers being between two and five. The most common way in which others helped was by looking after children so parents could go out in the evening or after school. Having someone to talk to also featured highly.

Table 7.1 Sources of help identified by parents

Family member who lives in another house	124
Resident partner	107
Neighbour(s)	100
Friend(s)	92
Family member within family home	46
Former partner/child's non-resident parent	25
Other	5

(N = 179)

Table 7.2 Kind of help provided by others

Let you go out in the evening	105
Look after children after school	103
Someone to talk to	98
Look after children in school holidays	76
Provide lifts	61
Other kinds of help	35

(N = 179)

Examples of other kinds of help included keeping an eye on children when they were out in the street, and help with practical tasks such as shopping and making children tea. Asked if they would like more help with parenting, only 19 per cent (N = 41) said they would. The proportion that would have liked more help was higher among people who had indicated that they had no help (28 per cent) and among lone parents (30 per cent). These relatively low figures could underlie a fear of not being seen as able to cope through admitting to need more help. Of those who wanted more help, about half referred to affordable childcare or clubs for children to attend when out of school. Apart from this, only a few respondents wanted additional help from services such as the police or education establishments.

Selective trusting of network members

In some areas in the UK the whole community is generally perceived to have a collective responsibility for children, underpinned by a community level of goodwill towards them. Ross (2002) has identified this as offering a web of protection. In the study areas this was not the case, since nearly all the parents regarded certain local people as representing a threat to young people. Additionally, young people themselves could be seen as threats when perceived as 'the wrong crowd'.

On the other hand, the building-up of safe networks among local people was a key strategy in maintaining children's safety as they pushed at boundaries and sought more independence. Neighbours, especially those with children of similar ages and extended family, were the adults most likely to be used to establish these networks. Most parents referred to people living nearby who they trusted to act for short periods as substitutes for themselves. These were often parents of the children's friends but sometimes other kinds of neighbour or relative. They acted as substitute parents with regard to providing a safe home, supervising and accompanying. For instance, a friend's parent might provide a lift for a child, either as part of a reciprocal arrangement or because the parents themselves did not run a car.

Below we see examples of how the parents of young people's friends can be used to develop safe networks that assist in the monitoring of young people.

> He goes to a rave on a Saturday and it comes out at half twelve. So wee Peter's Ma [friend's mother] will walk round ... so that works and if she cannae go, I'll walk round [and collect them]. (*Mother, Newhouse*) [The child in question was aged 11.]

> I'd say they are great neighbours. I mean a couple of them don't get as involved as they should I think. That's my only fault. I mean some of them, quite a lot, are nosey and that's great. I mean you get families who'll say 'They're too nosey, they're this an' that...' but I think nosey is good, because if your family isn't doing anything wrong you've got nothing to hide, y' know, kids will get up to mischief. (*Parent, Yardinch*)

This parent saw vigilance by neighbours as helping the local fabric of safety and not as intrusive – in her words, 'nosey is good'. This attitude could give parents intelligence about their children's exposure to risks. Neighbours and friends would often let parents know if they had been in trouble. Older siblings also often fulfilled roles in protecting, monitoring or reporting incidents that enabled parents to identify risks, as in the example below.

> Well it means he can't get up to too much, especially when he's got a sister that's 10 months older than him. So if he gets into any trouble or anything like that, she'll come and tell me. But Chelsea's always been a wee bit of a clipe [tell-tale], you know. Which is a good thing in a way, you know, basically she'll say, 'Mum, I don't like such and such he's going about with, he's not very good for him.' So she kind of watches him as well, she kinds of mothers him. They've all mothered him because he's the baby, so they've all kind of watched over him and make sure he's ok. (*Parent, Newhouse*)

Fewer children made reference to the role of trusted network members, but a number commented that older siblings, teachers and neighbours also looked out for them and kept them safe. One individual highlighted the fact that individuals other than mothers and fathers could 'parent'.

> *Interviewer:* Who keeps you safe, your mum and your dad or just your mum or just your dad?
> *Girl:* All my parents, my mum, my dad and my gran.
> (*Greenparks*)

Distrust of less familiar people

The corollary of placing trust in certain familiar people was that less well-known people were likely to evoke suspicion or anxiety. However the parents in the study offered both positive and negative evaluations of people living in their local neighbourhoods. To summarise the negative views, parents focused on the decline of 'community spirit' and the loosening of trust between people and the connections that trust fostered. During one particular discussion group held with 10-year-old boys and girls, there was a sense of parents protecting their children from certain other adults. In this interview, one individual discussed how he could only stay at a friend's house if the friend's mother was looking after him, and another mentioned that her parents only let her go with people she trusted. Additionally, a boy indicated his father would not let him stay with friends in case a stranger with bad intentions entered the house.

> *Boy*: If I ask to go somewhere with my friend he [father] would say no, or if I asked to stay with my friend he would just say no in case that person's mum had friends over, and you were playing PlayStation and they were in the toilet. And that person came in and tried to do stuff to you.
> *Interviewer*: Your dad won't let you stay at a friend's because of that?
> *Boy*: Yes, in case that person's dad had friends over.
> (*Foundry*)

A decline in trust could be seen as having a negative consequence on the resources at a community level that parents could draw upon. Threats to both short-term safety and long-term life chances were identified for their children. In relation to gangs for example, this could be related to the threat of gang violence in the short term and potential gang membership and the adoption of anti-school, anti-authority values in the long term. This coexisted with a perceived change in community spirit in which adults felt unable to challenge the anti-social behaviour of young people for fear of retribution on themselves. A connection between social problems and a decline in local trust and hence stock of social capital is illustrated by the following parent, views that were typical in the two most deprived areas in the study, Newhouse and Foundry.

> *Mother*: It has changed completely because the drug scene has taken over.
> *Interviewer*: How has the drug scene changed things?
> *Mother*: I mean out of every family you know there's a drug user amongst them. It's just too free and easy to get and that's why I'm worried about the young ones, as far as I know your first hit and that's you addicted.

> *Interviewer:* How does that change the feeling on the area and how people behave to one another?
>
> *Mother:* People aren't so friendly as they were. Years ago you could sit out, all the mothers sat out in the close and the weans played in each other's houses, that doesn't happen anymore.
> (*Newhouse*)

Such beliefs were reflected across the whole sample and were implicated in a perceived decline in trust. Drugs for example were not only seen as being a risk in themselves to the health and life chances of their children, but also drug users were seen to increase the risk of being a victim of crime. It also reflected a fear that parents could not simply trust people on the basis of their being a parent themselves or sharing a community (and of therefore being 'like us'). In Newhouse, the interviewer was told by one mother of how her son had things stolen from the house when peers called round. She said there was no recourse to resolution as 'their Mas are all junkies and they've just not got the time of day for you'. A different mother (in Foundry) said a friend of her 10-year-old daughter had stolen her purse when round at the house for a birthday party. She knew the girl's mother to be a heroin user, and speculated that not only did this mean she would not be able to resolve the issue, but further, that the girl had learnt the behaviour from her mother.

The good and bad parent: shaping the character of one's community through parenting

Central to the discourses of many correspondents about their own parenting was the notion of the bad other parent, who acted as a counterpoint to how parents considered themselves. Such 'bad' parents not only contributed to a decline in good neighbouring, but presented specific threats to respondents' own children, directly or through the bad influence of the children these parents were bringing up as. The drug-using parent was a common feature of pathologies portrayed in the communities in Foundry and Newhouse. In Greenparks however, residents were more likely to allude to parents who did not adequately supervise or monitor their children's whereabouts, perceived as another agent of community decline:

> In a lot of these cases the parents just don't know where their kids are at night and who they are with. We always know who our boy's out with and where he is and if he's going any further than the immediate streets, he's to come and tell us. (*Mother, Greenparks*)

As described in Chapter 5, parental monitoring was seen as not only fundamental to ideas of being a good parent, but was also identified as being beneficial on two levels. Firstly it was seen as an effective means of keeping young people out of trouble; secondly, and relevant to beliefs about community spirit, it was seen as making the community safer through providing a network of parents concerned for young people's welfare. As this involved the monitoring and reporting of young people's negative behaviour, a coalition of parents made the community safer for both young people and adults. It seems parents felt they could shape the character of the community they lived in through the parental monitoring of their own children and by being receptive to other parent's reports of their own children's transgressions of accepted behaviour. In this way, current policy movements towards punishing parents for not adequately supervising their children would have support in the communities we studied. However, it is important to re-emphasise that the sample of families in the research did not appear to include any parents who could be seen as 'bad parents' in the ways described.

Additionally, the views of parents who considered their own monitoring was effective and that of others was not did not take into account the agency of young people themselves (as discussed in Chapter 6) and how young people create space and time away from adult supervision. It is entirely feasible that the above parent only believes to know where and with whom the son is at all times.

Utilising existing resources and networks

Although many parents spoke of a decline in trust and reciprocity in the communities they lived in, there was also evidence of existing networks in parents' lives that did provide help and assistance. In addition to these networks there was also evidence of forms of trust which, if not being actively utilised for help and support, could form a backdrop of what was known and safe about an area. Most often the core of networks used by parents was extended family such as grandparents and the siblings of the parents themselves. Importantly however, support and sources of advice could come via links established by young people, in particular in the form of the parents of young people's friends who acted as useful sources of information and were identified as having similar aspirations and values.

Extended family

Family members represented sources of advice and support known and trusted by parents, or at least, sources of which parents knew for sure the limits of expectation and standards. Extended family members often contributed to the monitoring strategies of parents, and their homes provided safe places where parents believed they knew who and what their children would come into contact with. This was aided when parental siblings had children themselves, as the demands of reciprocity with regard to mutual help and advice were looser than for non-kin (Hill 2002). Also, franker negotiations about standards and expectations could be held with these extended family members. Parental siblings with older children would also provide useful sources of advice, as experienced parents who had seen many of the problems before:

> I've got my sister-in-law who's not far from me, she's got two older boys and Gary is identical to one of them. What Gary's doing at 13, he did when he was he was 13. It's quite good having that support, knowing that other folk have been there through it and, you know, you can go to them for advice. (*Newhouse*)

> Well according to my sister, he goes about with the wrong people! Don't get me wrong, some of them are fine but there's other ones that do get in to bother but she seems to think he likes that kind of lifestyle, it's appealing to him just now, it must just be like a kind of phase he's going through. (*Newhouse*)

A mother in Foundry told how she wished for respite help occasionally but felt it inappropriate to call upon neighbours or family friends. She saw this as a disadvantage that would have been remedied had her own family lived nearby.

Being known

Being known by other young people in the community was a very prominent feature of young people's accounts of staying safe, but figured less in interviews with parents. However, to be known by other young people in the area and learn about how to deal with and avoid risks, such as gang violence or drug and alcohol abuse, could well involve exposure to those risks, so many parents tended to ignore this as a possibility. Some parents did see it as having beneficial consequences however. In one instance a mother in Greenparks described how her daughter got out of a threatening situation when a member of a gang accosting her was able to identify her as sharing a mutual friend. In this instance the mother admitted that being 'known' got her out of a situation that might have turned nasty. It led the mother to question her own parenting strategy, which had up until that point involved insulating her daughter from the people and places which posed risks.

A development in one community that underlined how the benefits of being known combine with the exposure to risk it involves was a local educational reorganisation, which led to children from a much wider area going to the same secondary school. On the one hand it allowed young people to become friends through school with peers from different areas who previously would have viewed each other with mutual suspicion. However it posed an added dilemma for parents, as it increased potential risk when young people went to visit their friends further away, leaving the safety of their own scheme where they were known and unlikely to encounter trouble. Getting known and benefiting from the safety that this derives therefore involves taking risks.

In one of the areas the respondents were very aware of the bad reputation the neighbourhood had locally. Some of these parents recognised the risks but claimed they would not choose to move if offered somewhere else. When exploring the data for reasons that this was the case, one factor appeared to be that even when the risks were perceived as relatively high, parents' familiarity with the risks could to some extent alleviate their fear of them and help to manage the concerns.

> I don't know, I think it's just because we know everybody. Everybody you walk by you know, do you know what I mean? Don't get me wrong, I know people up in [another area] and all but it's just – it's a place I wouldn't like to stay, drugswise and ... it probably hasn't got any more drug users than this area but, it's just, all the junkies that walk about on my street – I know them all! (*Parent, Newhouse*)

Familiarity, it seemed, could imbue a feeling of safety of even the most risky situations and people.

> I think it's true the saying, 'Better the devil you know ...' you tend to know your neighbours and they know you, they've got their problems like everybody else but you know the strengths of each other. (*Parent, Newhouse*)

Parents viewed a mixture of good and bad within their local communities and social networks, and this range was carefully negotiated by parents in a manner that underlined the strategies identified in Chapter 5. Monitoring and open communication were seen as vital to facilitating young people's safe negotiation of their communities and its attendant risks. It helped parents to predict threats that might arise and to then pass on the knowledge of how to prepare their children for exposure to inevitable risk, as this father explains:

> If I'm parenting OK, if you're doing the right thing by them I don't think it would matter where they were brought up because – well, I was brought up here and I know a lot of people that have been brought up here and they're

fine and just, we've got good, everyday normal people. It's the minority that waste it, isn't it? I suppose there's good and bad everywhere. ... And although he's 13 I think at this age it's quite dodgy whether he'll go that road or that road, or he could get into the wrong company. But you can only keep explaining to them and talking to them. (*Parent, Newhouse*)

Conclusion

Most parents felt well supported in their role. Other parents, friends and neighbours often also acted as part of a safety network looking out for and after children. The main wish for additional help centred on childcare and children's leisure provision. Some respondents condemned other '*bad*' parents, which they saw as contributing to a decline in community integration and the increase in risky behaviours locally. However, the evidence suggests that being 'known' could mitigate the risks in the minds of respondents regarding the parents they worried about; being a '*bad*' parent often meant being an *unknown* parent.

8.   Hopes and aspirations

This chapter explores the views parents and young people had of their future career aspirations. These hopes and aspirations are set against the backdrop of their communities, as both sets of respondents balanced the perceived obstacles to future success with perceived opportunities. The findings have implications for schools and policies for increasing access into further and higher education. Whilst both parents and young people had aspirations in accordance with policies to extend educational opportunities to greater numbers, the weaker social capital available means there was not a level playing field compared with children from more advantaged areas.

Parents' hopes for their children

When invited to discuss their thoughts and hopes for their children's futures, parents concentrated on one or more of four life domains – education and employment, health, personality, and lifestyle. These were seen as interconnected, for example, with a child's character influencing job prospects, and both having lifestyle consequences. Concern with education and jobs was key but not an exclusive part of parents' aspirations for their children.

A better life

Many parents talked of giving their children a better life than they had. Many of their comments were premised on limitations in their own lives, so that they wished for their children's lives to improve compared with their own:

> I want them to have some of the things we never had ... to have a good shot at life. (*Parent, Newhouse*)

Education and employment

Usually parents saw doing well in education and employment as key to doing better. On the whole parents had high aspirations for their children's education. Figure 8.1 shows that for the parents who completed questionnaires, only about a quarter expected their children to leave school by Year 5. Just under half expected their children to go on to further or higher education, and an additional one in 10 thought they would leave formal education after Year 6.

Young people who completed questionnaires were asked when they thought they would leave school, and the majority felt they would stay in school past the age of compulsory education. Most believed parental aspirations for them were similar (Tables 8.1 and 8.2):

Figure 8.1 Age at which parents believe their children will leave education

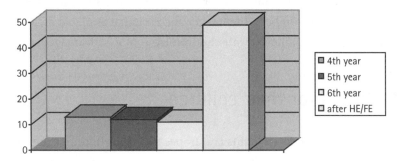

Table 8.1 When are you planning to leave school? (Young people)

	N	%
At the end of S4	43	17
At the end of S5	62	24
At the end of S6	136	52

Table 8.2 When do your parents think you will leave school?

	N	%
At the end of S4	49	19
At the end of S5	48	18
At the end of S6	142	55

Table 8.3 What are you planning to do when you leave home?

Plans	N	%	Rank
Go to college	139	54	1
Go to university	125	48	2
Find a part-time job	119	46	3
Find a full-time job	87	34	4
Take a year out	29	11	5
Be unemployed	6	2	6

(Respondents could tick more than one)

Just under half the young people hoped to go to university (Table 8.3), which in view of their backgrounds is sadly a proportion unlikely to be fulfilled.

Parents' hopes for their children's future employment

Parents also saw work type as crucial for children's prospects. 'Good jobs' were seen as those that not only offered more pay but offered more opportunities for children to have lives different from their parents. Parents recognised the value of education in achieving these ends.

> A better environment to live in, a better job, more money and more, more everything than what we could get when we were young. I mean there's things out there for him if he uses his head at school. (*Parent, Newhouse*)

Although they often had high aspirations for their children, parents did not usually express definite wishes for them to take up specific jobs, but supported young people's choices. Commonly, parents described helping young people to develop an understanding of their strengths and to choose jobs that would suit their perceived abilities and would ultimately fulfil them. The emphasis was on individualisation, rather than following or escaping the previous generation's type of work (cf. Furlong and Cartmel 1997).

Some parents, who saw their children as academic, did cite traditional jobs requiring higher education such as accountancy or law. However, perceived academic ability was not the only guide to future careers. Some parents recognised other qualities that could be a basis for certain career choices, and cited their children's musical or creative ability, their caring nature, love of animals or ability to get on with people.

In the following examples, parents pointed to highly differentiated and personalised characteristics or interests as relevant:

> [On her son becoming a policeman] And he would be good at that because he's dead observant, he's really, really observant. But he's not very academic, that's the problem. (*Mother, Foundry*)

> [On her son's plans to join the Army] You don't need to be the brain of Britain, as long as you can use your hands, they'll give you a trade. So I hope he will join the Army, he's talking about going into the TA just now ... Rachel's good with her hands, she's an artist, she sits and draws for hours, so I think she will end up doing something like that. (*Mother, Foundry*)

Young people's career choices

Young people had a diverse range of careers in mind. Most wanted to follow occupations (for example, football, acting) that were different from their parents, and quite a few aspired to join professions such as teachers, scientists, vets and lawyers. Often work was still some way off, so they were usually more sure about their plans in the shorter term. For instance, some spoke of improvement at school such as a higher grade in a certain subject.

When talking about what jobs they would like to do as adults, young people mainly drew on sources close to themselves. They mentioned jobs that were extensions of activities they enjoyed or were good at or talked about jobs that adults they knew already did. Becoming a football player was a popular choice among boys and reflects this first category. Other choices included becoming a designer, driving lorries or taxis, or becoming a mechanic (for those who liked cars), becoming dancers or actors (for those who enjoyed drama classes), air steward (likes flying) or becoming a veterinarian (for those who liked animals). Some young people identified following careers that reflected certain values they had, such as having a strong sense of justice (lawyer), wanting to improve safety within their own community (police officer) or having a compassionate nature (medical profession).

Some job wishes were related to what young people had seen on television. A few who wanted to become lawyers cited popular television shows such as *CSI* as a reason. None of the small number who mentioned becoming a lawyer actually knew anyone in their families and beyond who was already in the occupation. When an occupation was chosen because they knew someone doing it already, the options were less glamorous than television lawyers, except for one girl who through her dancing classes, had become acquainted with a professional dancer. Options in the category of known occupations covered things such as working in a job centre, mechanic, bricklaying and lorry driving. Exposure to familiar adults in the chosen field of work helped the young person to see the benefits and develop skills, which encouraged them to follow suit. A 13-year-old boy discussing the role of his mother's partner, who was a bricklayer, illustrates this:

> He showed me how to put the slabs together and other things. He says it's good to do ... it's good because he gets to be a lot of places and saves you from just walking about drinking and all that all time. You are better off having a job ... He says one day he is going to build a wee thing with me, he doesnae know what but he is gonna try and help me wae it. (*Boy, Newhouse*)

This boy had also taken bricklaying classes at school, which he had enjoyed. In the following extract, a girl is talking about following her older sister in becoming a beautician:

> My big sister, she has gone through college and she has done it. She practised on dummy models first and then she got to do it on real people ... she practises on me and then I'll do it to her. (*Girl, Newhouse*)

This young person could utilise her sister's knowledge of the training procedure to access college courses. Having such family members or other social contacts already in certain jobs could assist in providing realistic appraisals of the job suitability and potential disadvantages as well as attractions. The girl who was friendly with a professional dancer had become aware of the difficult side of the profession and adapted her expectations accordingly:

> I do like Irish dancing but I wouldn't want to do it all the time really. I would like to be a teacher so that I could keep in with it but just for a couple of nights a week. Like when you become a professional dancer it's like going away for a year and not seeing your family and I would miss my family ... I know someone who became a dancer and she really likes it but she says it's really hard work and they make you become really, really skinny and I don't want to go on a diet or that. (*Girl, Foundry*)

Staying or going

For some parents moving on was likely to require their children moving away. They envisaged their children going to parts of Scotland with greater opportunities, or even other countries. This resulted from parental perceptions of the local areas as offering more risk than opportunity. Even parents who were optimistic about their children's employment and other prospects after leaving school believed that moving away was vital to avoid the continuing risks from the character of the local area and residents, such as falling in with the wrong crowd.

Children's thoughts on staying or moving

Young people were divided on the issue of moving away. Many saw this as a positive thing and cited negative aspects of their communities as a reason for this.

> [Explaining why he would not stay in the area as an adult] I wouldnae have job anyway – that would be one thing. (*Boy, Yardinch*)

Other young people with specific career aspirations thought about moving away to pursue specific aims. A girl who wanted to be a hairdresser identified a perceived lack of hairdressing salons in her local area [Foundry] as reason to move away.

Besides limited work opportunities, others mentioned the violence and gang activity that was seen to be a particular characteristic of the area. Below a girl talks of a nearby seaside town she envisages living in when she is older. Notions of her safety are paramount in her aspiring to live there.

> It's just a wee place, it's a beach, it's not far away, there's a fun fair, right beside the train station. That's where I'd feel safe. That's a good place to go because there are no gangs and no fighting. I'd be all right there. (*11-year-old girl, Yardinch*)

Places that young people had visited on holiday also featured as possible destinations to move to, often reflecting the happy times that had been spent there (for example, Florida, Cornwall and Wales). Young people also mentioned places where members of their family lived, again citing the familiarity of people they knew there.

Yet others did not want to leave despite their recognition of the area's perceived problems. The two main factors were the desire to be close to their families and their familiarity with the place.

> I want to stay in Yardinch because it is where my family is, if you wanted to go away, it is because the hooligans are here. (*Child, Yardinch*)

One young person believed he would move to another city but said his family would go with him.

When children and young people were asked in the questionnaire whether they would be living in Scotland when they were 18, two-thirds (65 per cent) replied 'yes'.

Personal qualities

Parents spoke of personality traits in their children that they could influence both as aspirations in their own right and as prerequisites for a better life. Parents were asked what kind of traits and characteristics young people needed to achieve their aspirations. On the one hand, self-reliance and the ability to work for themselves were seen as important, but social skills were valued too. Some parents described how they had always hoped that their children could fit in and mix with others. Such qualities could help avoid succumbing to perceived risks of adolescence. Keeping out of trouble in the teen years was thought to be crucial for life chances.

> I think I've done OK so far but it could all go down the slippery slope because he's turning a teenager. Just to get a good job will be OK, I don't want him turning into a wee toe rag, one of they wee loud things that you see running about the streets. (*Parent, Newhouse*)

Parental strategies to improve young people's futures

Some parents felt it was important that they themselves were seen to work and that this set a good example, especially if their working was seen to be connected to things young people enjoyed such as holidays or material goods. Parents would also use their children's desire for material things as a means of spurring them on in school, by making the link between being able to have things they want and having a good job. Praise and encouragement were seen as critical inputs from parents that could interact with the opportunities found in school and outside interests. It seems that having high self-esteem and realistic self-appraisals were seen as axiomatic for success. Some parents were aware that a combination of opportunities and supportive, facilitative parenting increased the chances of success:

> You need to listen to them and make sure they are comfortable with their going to school and things like that. If they are going to clubs or anything like that, make sure they are settled in and they've not got any problems they are hiding away. (*Parent, Newhouse*)

> I try to prepare her for life, people might say things to you to be cruel but don't feel that what they say is true, don't let it make you feel bad ... I want

> her to have the confidence to make her own choices, if you know what I
> mean. Confident enough to be confident. (*Parent, Newhouse*)

Encouraging hobbies was seen as one key means of improving young people's
futures, as the resilience literature has identified (Gilligan 2001).

Parental encouragement of participation in organised activities was not only
regarded as an effective way of keeping young people's busy and safe, but as a means
of enhancing future prospects. Hobbies and out-of-school activities were seen as
drawing out strengths innate in young people, and believed to foster character traits
such as determination and consistency through keeping up hobbies over time.

> You know exactly what your kids are up to, that's why we've always
> encouraged our kids to be involved in the Boy's Brigade, Girl's Brigade,
> football, activities and things run by local organisations. (*Parent, Greenparks*)

The following parent explicitly linked individual and societal goals by reference to
citizenship:

> It takes the kids off the streets and it also teaches them good principles as
> well. Even the likes of football, we teach our kids good principles, it's not
> just about being a good footballer, it's also about being a good citizen ...
> you can teach them about respect ... you can influence them a little and
> actually give them a bit of discipline. (*Parent, Greenparks*)

Obstacles

The perceived limitations of the area were frequently cited as thwarting ambition,
through the paucity of facilities and the danger of imitating others with a
disapproved of lifestyle:

> There's nothing in this area for kids to do and it's when kids are bored
> that they are going to get into trouble. If they had more youth clubs and
> things like that for the kids, you know keep them off the streets. Because
> let's be honest, a lot of the parents around here are drug users or whatever,
> they're just going to fall into their mother's and father's footsteps.
> (*Parent, Foundry*)

As noted in Chapter 5, outside activities could be prohibitively expensive. Providing
the necessary financial and practical support often relied on sacrifices by parents and
extended kin.

Some parents who believed their children's lives were not on the track for success felt that they were in part to blame, especially when they compared themselves to other parents.

> It hasn't worked out the way I'd hoped. He's having problems in school. So it's hard, you feel as though you failed. My sister's got three kids but hers are fine. (*Parent, Newhouse*)

This mother believed that doing well at school was crucial to success in later life, so thought her son's dislike of school was 'ruining it for himself'. She saw his main strength as self-confidence (though this sometimes became 'cheek') and being good on his computer. Asked how it might be possible to bring out his strengths to benefit him in the transition to adulthood, she explored the idea that a non-academic route may be more appropriate for him.

> Maybe school's not just for him, but maybe when he leaves school he can find something to bring out his good side. He likes his DJ thing, he sits in his room with his decks. And as well he likes, he liked his construction course, well he liked bits of it, not all of it though.
> (*Parent, individual interview, Newhouse*)

Such combinations of observation, practical training and informal advice available in social networks helped ground occupational plans in first-hand knowledge of what was entailed.

Conclusions: Implications for young people's resilience

Having ambitions and aspirations is important for children, because having a sense of purpose and belief in the future have been identified as key components of childhood resilience (Bernard 1991; Gilligan 1997; Rutter 1999; Gilligan 2001; Shapiro and Levendosky 1999). It also provides motivation to do well at school and allows young people to see schoolwork as having relevance beyond the day-to-day experience of it. That parents have shared aspirations for their children is also vital for supporting children and giving them a sense that their aims are realistic and achievable. It is also noteworthy how parental appraisals of their children's abilities and individual strengths were factored into their estimations of future occupations, showing that parents often had the interests of their children's well-being and happiness at the core of their aspirations for them.

However, these aspirations were also clearly formed within the context of the areas in which they lived. This highlights ecological influences on finding work and sustaining careers. Research in both the United States and the United Kingdom has highlighted how social ties can help people access employment opportunities (Jack and Gill 2003; Pavis and others 2000). Few of the parents interviewed had experience of college or university education themselves, and they would therefore be at a disadvantage when it came to advising and supporting during the application process, or in the transition to higher education, where young people from less advantaged backgrounds are over-represented in the drop-out rates, often for cultural reasons (Forsyth and Furlong 2003).

Parents and extended kin and peer networks in these communities were best equipped to support young people in decision-making processes in less prestigious careers based less on academic qualifications. Consequently schools and other agencies involved in education would have to offer additional support to young people (and their families) who are aspiring to higher education. That the task of helping young people achieve educational ambitions is a family-centred exercise in middle-class families has long been identified (for example, Allatt 1993), and while formal qualifications will always be seen as an indication of *individual* ability, recognising the family and network impact on their likelihood of success should be a future focus of educational policy in raising attainment levels.

9. Parenting in high-risk communities and promoting young people's resilience

The two linked studies described in this report were carried out in four neighbourhoods in the west of Scotland representing different types of urban environment, but all characterised by high levels of unemployment, crime and children receiving free school meals. A total of 144 individual interviews were carried out (84 with parents and 60 with children) and 33 focus groups (17 with parents and 16 with children). The children ranged in age from eight to 14. In addition, questionnaires were completed by wider samples from the same areas, 231 by parents and 259 by children. The sample was recruited via schools to achieve a 'normative' sample, that is, ordinary families rather than ones known to official agencies because of material or other difficulties.

Summary of key points from the study

Most parents and children had a positive view of the areas they lived in, which was mostly dependent on a network of supportive relationships comprising kin and other parents for the adults and peers for the children. At the same time, the main perceived threats to children's well-being, in the eyes of both parents and children, were also mostly produced by other people rather than dangerous physical environments. They referred in particular to territorial teenage gangs and adults affected by drug and alcohol misuse.

The parents in the study were very concerned to keep their children safe and promote their development. There was much evidence that they supported values with an emphasis on democracy and communication within family processes and individualised career choices.

Ideas about risk and threat were key organising principles of daily life and were closely related to the local context, in particular the interaction between person, place, time and activity (cf. Harden and others 2000; Crawshaw 2002). Safety responses of both parents and young people were based on detailed knowledge of these contextual factors.

The use of organised activity was a strong theme, and was revealed to be multi-functional, providing safety, approved company and skill development. In this regard, the use of organised activity mirrored more middle-class households (Allatt 1993), with an extra element of community risk etched on to the safety enhancing aspect.

Young people were also concerned to keep themselves and their friends safe and look out for each other. Not only did they share their parents' views on risk and safety but they also showed a degree of agency in developing strategies within the peer group and as individuals.

Particularly when older, young people were sometimes willing and able to ignore or subvert parental rules and strategies. However, young people by this time were highly conscious of safety issues and displayed knowledge of how to keep themselves safe, often substituting peer support for parents.

Parents sought to protect their children from the effects of low income. Their strategies for achieving this showed a high degree of creativity and underlined resilience enhancing strategies. However, these strategies did not prevent social exclusion, as attested by the large number of children on free school meals and parental fears about their children fitting in with their peer group and the potential consequences of this.

The capacity to fulfil aspirations is highly dependent on the availability of appropriate resources. Parents often had high aspirations for their children, but many appeared not to have adequate knowledge and experience to support these, for example, with regard to accessing and supporting higher education.

Despite these areas being characterised by high levels of anti-social behaviour, the parents saw such behaviour as detrimental to their own quality of life and their children's life chances. These parents may well be inclined to support policies designed to tackle anti-social behaviour as they are likely to see them aimed at 'other' parents, who they also blame for the deterioration in civil life.

Promoting young people's resilience in high-risk communities

In this section the risks and strategies associated with parenting and childhood in disadvantaged communities are explored with reference to the concept of resilience.

The central meaning of resilience is doing well despite adversity. In this study, the adversities most stressed by informants were social environmental, though limited income was a factor that both resulted in their residing in areas with several major threats to children and affected parents' capacities to raise children safely and positively despite the environmental hazards. While we had no external evidence about family functioning, the majority of families in the study appeared to be coping well.

It has been argued that resilience is best seen not as a personality trait or outcome but as an interactive process between individual or family and features of their environment (Rutter and Smith 1995; Gilligan 2001; Schofield 2001). This study illuminated the processes by which both parents and young people actively managed the interaction of risks and protective factors that affect vulnerability and resilience. When depicting their local areas, both adult and child respondents showed detailed awareness of a range of immediate risks to children's safety and well-being, particularly associated with aggression by teenage gangs and adults with drink or drug problems, which they sought to guard against. Equally important, though often more implicit, were threats to children's long-term life chances, exemplified by the dangers of children being drawn into anti-social behaviour or crime and restricted horizons in their experiences, aspirations and opportunities.

Parenting and resilience

A number of texts have identified parental characteristics that promote prospective resilience in young people. These have been listed as warmth, responsiveness and stimulation; providing adequate and consistent role models; harmony between parents; spending time with children; promoting constructive use of leisure; consistent guidance; and structure and rules during adolescence (Hill and others 2004). The findings in this report point to how the last three factors help young people navigate high-risk environments and also indicate some of the ways in which this can be supported. Information from both parents and children has shown the vital importance of close monitoring and clear rules, as previous research found (for example, Laybourn 1986). However, the data have also revealed that the way that parents negotiate this is crucial.

In communities where the risks associated with a failure of children to follow adult guidance are high (resulting in drug and alcohol use, peer activity likely to lead into trouble with the police, exclusion from education) the risk of experimenting with democratic parenting styles might seem a high-risk strategy. Yet the accounts of children and parents confirmed the value of communicative, democratic family processes. In their view, this was not simply a *desirable* parenting style but the most *effective*. The great majority of both generations recognised the need and value of open communication concerning the time, place and nature of risks and the associated rules for protecting children and promoting their prospects.

Such parenting styles had developed through interaction with children in households and engagement with the risks associated with their communities in both adults' and children's worlds. These risks and opportunities are also set against secular changes in society such as increased consumerism, individualisation and recognition of children's participatory and autonomy rights. Not only do democratic parenting styles offer relative resilience in these situations, they also incorporate these newer considerations.

At the same time, a key strategy adopted by many of the parents was to encourage or insist on their children's involvement in adult-organised activities. These served dual functions of offering safe recreation and developing life-chance-enhancing skills and connections (that is, they built social capital, which in turn is likely to engender resilience). Yet these activities incurred monetary and time costs, so this option was to some degree reliant on low-cost availability. Also, if used exclusively, this approach could become in tension with children's wishes for unsupervised peer association.

Children's perspectives

The consensus between children and adults about the scale and identification of risk was striking, and partly responsible for the large degree of harmony between parents and young people. It facilitated the practice of monitoring young people's whereabouts, associations and activities for example, with young people understanding and appreciating why it was necessary. When children were outside the purview of trusted adults, then distance monitoring mechanisms were dependent on children's agency and cooperation (for example, reporting back, coming in on time, maintaining mobile phone contact). This is not to claim young people were always forthcoming or completely honest, as understandably they wanted to carve out some autonomy in their own sphere, but it reveals they understood the same parameters of risk and safety as their parents. When young people did go against their parents' established boundaries and chose not to inform them, this did not usually mean a rejection of their parent's estimations of risk and safety, but rather a transferring of the responsibility for caution on to themselves *and their friends* on these occasions. As young people are often the experts on their spheres of experience the argument could tentatively be made that they are often better placed to judge, though Valentine (2004) warns that a sense of invulnerability may cloud their judgements.

There was certainly evidence that at times the main reason for children disregarding or subverting parental rules was concern about embarrassment among peers. Even then this may allow young people to access the opportunities for development within their communities that sit among the risks and hazards. The point is that they *know* these places, associations or activities carry risk and knowing this they can more safely navigate them in a semi-independent manner. This would fit previous analyses of children's resilience in high-risk communities, where the encouragement of autonomy has been part of a raft of resilience-enhancing characteristics (Gilligan 2001), with success more likely when parents do not necessarily control the external world but provide young people with an orientation toward it that acts as a means of management (Furstenberg and others 1999).

Although parents were often central in developing links with the external world that were part of this management, the strategies young people instigated should not be overlooked. Collective responses to these threats, utilising the peer group, were often central, and engagement with the community was necessary to safely navigate the risks. Young people therefore expressed the same concern and dilemma as their parents: how to safely engage in social networks that offer protection without falling foul of the risks.

A key message from the research was the positive role of peers, which the adults often underestimated. Friends helped provide knowledge of risks and safety, support and reciprocal monitoring. Their presence was often protective when moving through risky places, though there is a danger that being and moving in groups is interpreted as threatening by adults or other children. Hence being popular was both an end in itself and a means of safely navigating high-risk communities. This makes the consequences for being unpopular particularly high, in that the peer group was a key means of establishing safety.

A worrying trend may be the possibility of unpopularity being associated with social disadvantage in other spheres, as childhoods become more material in focus. From the data collected, not having the right clothes, gadgets or other consumer projects was connected to social pariah status, though this was emphasised more by adults than the children. Other young people also presented obstacles to successful association and use of spaces in these communities. Gang activity restricted movements of young people but so can overzealous adult fears of anti-social behaviour and a shortage of safe opportunities for young people to congregate outside of school.

Engaging with the community or dividing the community?

How parents and young people engage with their communities is a key finding in relation to resilience. The differentiation of spaces and people individually or in groups into safe and unsafe was an essential aspect of resilience strategies which, whilst effective for the individual families concerned, may actually detract from social cohesion in the community (Sibley 1995). The concept of 'normative dissonance' has been used to describe the discrepancy between how people see themselves and how they see the areas they live (Popay and others 2003). It claims that when people view areas as not reflecting their own values and aspirations it is accompanied with a withdrawal from engagement in that community as a means of protecting self-images and also avoiding the stress involved in potential conflicts or 'neighbourhood incivilities' (Airey 2003).

In this data there was evidence that parents in particular distinguished between the 'good' and the 'bad' areas, and offered justifications for their categorisation on the basis of the people's behaviour there. Categorisation of area was fine-grained and helped most parents feel confident in their parenting, despite the high level of perceived risks locally. However, it also had a 'dark' side in that this process of differentiation would tend to cut off families who were living in the places that many parents interviewed thought should be avoided. Such families, with the greatest risks facing them, would thereby be excluded from the social networks and community-level processes that offer resilience-enhancing characteristics.

Among young people, gang activity and territoriality also threatened community and network resources that could otherwise offer protection. Not only did this create no-go areas for children from other 'territories', but sometimes gangs were perceived to have command of certain community resources such as leisure centres, which then came to be seen by parents as part of an alternative geography of potential trouble spots. Whereas this mental mapping was useful and assisted in the safe navigation of neighbourhoods, it underlines the fact that simply giving communities resources does not mean all residents get to access them safely and equally.

The issue of territoriality was not alone in preventing access, because issues of transport and entry costs were also critical, as were organising household 'carescapes' to allow the ferrying of young people to and from such locations. A potential strength to counterbalance this was that schools were seen as safe spaces where gang activity was largely suspended. This suggests that the policy of integrating schools better into the community and providing evening access for leisure and community activity could serve such communities well.

Policy implications

The data collected highlights how potential assistance for those living and parenting in high-risk communities cuts across a broad range of policy areas.

Housing policy

The importance of social networks highlights the advantage of being able to choose where one lives. It is therefore vital to support parents in disadvantaged communities to have a degree of choice in where they are housed, which is mostly within the social rented sector. It is also vital that parents feel there are other parents within their neighbourhood with whom they share similar aims and aspirations, so that tasks and knowledge of parenting can be shared. While this cannot be engineered and homogenous communities would reduce social capital in other ways, facilitating the housing of families and parents together in communities can enhance stocks of social capital relevant to successful parenting.

Justice policy

Anti-social behaviour (ASB) has become a central policy concern in recent times, and one that intersects with regeneration policies and (with the introduction of parenting orders) family policy. In this study ASB of both young people and adults was a concern to children as well as adults. There is a tendency to view young people as the cause of ASB and adults and civil safety as the victims. Irrespective of the underlying causes, the data showed how young people's safety is often compromised, and that it is just as often the behaviours of adults (relating to legal-age drinking and drug misuse) that are viewed as the risks to safety.

Our findings support a recent Joseph Rowntree Foundation report that parents on the whole monitor and supervise their children (Stace and Roker 2004) and therefore already parent in a manner government policies encourage. Stace and Roker's research was with 'ordinary' families (those not in contact with statutory agencies) from diverse socio-economic backgrounds. Our research sends the same message from families with backgrounds characterised by socio-economic hardship: the very geographical areas where ASB is seen as a policy priority.

One way through which policies could assist parents in the task of parenting is though initiatives to facilitate and support the development of the parental networks utilised to gain the knowledge required for keeping children safe. Social networks can exclude as much as they include, however, and the problem for some parents can be of being unable to access these parental networks, especially if the parent has been labelled with the tag 'bad parent' by other parents (often on the basis of residence as discussed above). A parent-centred response to juvenile behaviour problems could work to help integrate socially excluded parents into safety enhancing informal networks where they can learn of safe activities for young people and develop reciprocal arrangements with other parents. Ensuring safe and low-cost access to organised activities is another prime means of preventing children from becoming the victims or perpetrators of anti-social behaviour and bullying.

Education and employment policy

The prominent role played by schools in these communities was clear in the data. Parents and young people alike spoke of schools positively on the whole, though there could be problems with communication between parents and schools over problem behaviour. As most parents actively seek to monitor young people's behaviour, teachers should support this ambition by communicating early with the home over matters of problem behaviour and assume that most parents will respond positively.

Schools could also play a key role in communities where territorialism is a problem. There was some evidence of schools overcoming territorial loyalties and easing tensions between gangs. Schools are also key resources in communities, and links between parents could also be strengthened through the continued opening of schools to the wider community outside of the school day.

Good education and employment opportunities were recognised as essential to enable people to navigate high-risk communities. Parents and young people displayed a range of aspirations and an understanding of the importance of further and higher education for success in the adult labour market. However, when it came to making realistic assessments of the processes and aptitudes required for success, both children and parents displayed more detailed understanding about lower-status jobs known through their social networks. This suggests that without the support and guidance of schools, young people would have realistic access only to a limited range of career options already represented in their community. Schools could provide more support and information for careers beyond local employment opportunities. The resilience strategies displayed by parents and young people relied upon the young people being seen to have a stake in their futures that was worth protecting against the risks of alcohol and drug abuse and falling in with the wrong crowd. This further underlines the necessity to support access to quality employment in disadvantaged communities.

The way in which certain parents struggled to manage on low incomes and tried hard to avoid debt for fear of not being able to afford repayments highlights difficulties that their children might face if offered a place in higher education and when considering student loans.

Community and regeneration policy

Parents and families were shown to be active in building social capital in communities characterised by a high degree of risk and a lack of trust. These processes, designed to keep their own children safe, can assist community regeneration by increasing feelings of safety for all and creating networks that foster trust and reciprocity. However, certain resources are needed to assist this, such as amenities and spaces for young people to socialise and mix, with relatively light supervision, and opportunities for parents to meet and have shared reference points. Many parents complained of a lack of adult supervised activity for young people in their communities, which were seen as lacking not only resources such as physical buildings for community use, but also adult volunteers. Policies could be put in place to encourage volunteering among adults that can improve the safety of young people living in high-risk areas and also increase social capital. This could also have the effect of reducing territorial tensions that underpin gang activity in the same manner as with schools.

It is also vital to incorporate children and young people's viewpoints in planning. They are often omitted from 'the community' or seen as enemies of it (Brent 2001; Hill and Wright 2003), but are as much a part of community life as adults with valuable understandings to contribute.

References

Airey, L (2003) *Locating Health and Illness: A study of women's experiences in two contrasting Edinburgh neighbourhoods.* PhD thesis. Edinburgh: University of Edinburgh.

Allatt, P 'Becoming privileged: The role of family processes', in Bates, I and Riseborough, G (eds) (1993) *Youth and Inequality.* Buckingham: Open University Press.

Backett-Milburn, K and others (2003) 'Contrasting lives, contrasting views? Understandings of health inequalities from children in differing social circumstances', *Social Science and Medicine,* 57, 613–23.

Backett-Milburn, K and Harden, J (2004) 'How children and their families construct and negotiate risk, safety and danger', *Childhood,* 11, 4, 429–47.

Backett-Milburn, K and others (2004) *Life In Low Income Families in Scotland: Research report.* Edinburgh: Scottish Executive.

Baldwin, AL and others 'Stress-resistant families and stress-resistant children', in Rolf, J and others (eds) (1990) *Risk and Protective Factors in the Development of Psychopathology.* Cambridge: Cambridge University Press.

Baron, S, Field, J and Schuller, T (eds) (2000) *Social Capital: Critical perspectives.* Oxford: Oxford University Press.

Baumrind, D (1978) 'Parental disciplinary patterns and social competence in children', *Youth and Society,* 9, 229–76.

Baumrind, D and Black, AE (1967) 'Socialization practices associated with dimensions of competence in pre-school boys and girls', *Child Development,* 38, 2, 291–327.

Bernard, B (1991) *Fostering Resiliency in Kids: Protective factors in the family, school and community.* Portland, OR: Northwest Regional Education Laboratory.

Borland, M and others (1998) *Middle Childhood.* London: Jessica Kingsley.

Bott, E (1957) *Family and Social Network.* London: Tavistock.

Bradshaw, J and Mayhew, E (eds) (2005) *The Well-being of Children in the UK.* London: Save the Children.

Brent, J (2001) 'Trouble and tribes: young people and community', *Youth and Policy,* 73, 1–19.

Bronfenbrenner, U (1979) *The Ecology of Human Development.* Cambridge, Mass.: Harvard University Press.

Byrne, D (1999) *Social Exclusion*. Buckingham: Open University Press.

Coleman, JS (1988) 'Social capital in the creation of human capital', *American Journal of Sociology*, 94, s95–s120.

Collings, WA and others 'Parenting during middle childhood', in Bornstein, MH (ed) (1995) *Handbook of Parenting: Children and parenting*. Hillsdale, NJ: Lawrence Erlbaum.

Crawshaw, P (2002) 'Negotiating space in the risky community', *Youth and Policy*, 74, 59–72.

Dixey, R (1999) 'Keeping children safe: The effect on parents' daily lives and psychological well-being', *Journal of Health Psychology*, 4, 45–67.

Fletcher, A and others (1995) 'The company they keep: relation of adolescents' adjustment and behavior to the friends' perceptions of authoritative parenting in the social network', *Developmental Psychology*, 31, 300–10.

Flick, U (1998) *An Introduction to Qualitative Research*. London: Sage.

Fonagy, P and others (1994) 'The theory and practice of resilience', *Journal of Child Psychology and Psychiatry*, 35, 2, 231–57.

Forsyth, A and Furlong, A (2003) *Losing Out? Socioeconomic disadvantage and experience in further and higher education*. Bristol: Policy Press.

Furlong, A and Cartmel, F (1997) *Young People and Social Change: Individualization and risk in the age of high modernity*. Open University Press: Buckingham.

Furstenberg, F and others (1999) *Managing to Make It: Urban families and adolescent success*. Chicago: University of Chicago Press.

Ghate, D and Hazel, N (2002) *Parenting in Poor Environments: Stress, support and coping*. London: Jessica Kingsley.

Giddens, A (1992) *The Transformation of Intimacy: Sexuality, Love and Eroticism in Contemporary Societies*. Cambridge: Polity.

Gilligan, R (1997) 'Beyond permanence? The importance of resilience in child placement practice and planning', *Adoption and Fostering*, 21, 1, 12–20.

Gilligan, R 'Promoting resilience in children in foster care', in Kelly, G and Gilligan, R (2000) *Issues in Foster Care*. London: Jessica Kingsley.

Gilligan, R 'Promoting positive outcomes for children in need: the assessment of protective factors', in Horvath, J (2001) *The Child's World*. London: Jessica Kingsley.

Glennerster, H and others (2004) *One Hundred Years of Poverty and Policy*. York: Joseph Rowntree Foundation.

Hammen, C 'Risk and protective factors for children of depressed parents' in Luthar, SS (2003) *Resilience and Vulnerability: Adaptation in the context of childhood adversities*. Cambridge: Cambridge University Press.

Harden, J and others (2000) 'Scary faces, scary places: children's perceptions of risk and safety', *Family and Social Environment*, 59, 1, 12–22.

Hennessy, E and Heary, C 'Exploring children's views through focus groups', in Greene, S and Hogan, S (2005) *Researching Children's Experience: Approaches and methods.* London: Sage.

Hill, M (ed) (2002) *Shaping Childcare Practice in Scotland.* London: BAAF.

Hill, M 'Social networks, social capital and social work education', in Labonte-Roset, C, Marynowicz-Hetka, E and Szmagalski, J (2003) *Social Work Education and Practice in Today's Europe.* Katowice: Slask.

Hill, J and Wright, G (2003) 'Youth, community safety and the paradox of inclusion', *The Howard Journal,* 42, 3, 282–97.

Hill, M and others (2004) *Parenting and Resilience.* York: Joseph Rowntree Foundation.

Holman, B (1998) *Faith in the Poor.* Oxford: Lion.

Hood, S and others (1996) *Children, Parents and Risk.* London: Social Science Research Unit, Institute of Education.

Horwath, J (ed) (2001) *The Child's World.* London: Jessica Kingsley.

Howard, S and Johnston, B (2000) 'What makes the difference? Children and teachers talk about resilient outcomes for children 'at risk'', *Educational Studies,* 26, 3, 321–37.

Jack, G (2000) 'Ecological influences on parenting and child development', *British Journal of Social Work,* 30, 6, 703–36.

Jack, G and Gill, O (2003) *The Missing Side of the Triangle: Assessing the importance of family and environmental factors in the lives of children.* Ilford: Barnardo's.

James, A and Prout, A (eds) (1998) *Constructing and Reconstructing Childhood.* London: Falmer Press.

Laybourn, A (1986) 'Traditional strict working class parenting – an undervalued system', *British Journal of Social Work,* 16, 6, 625–44.

Maccoby, E and Martin, J 'Socialisation in the context of the family: parent-child interactions', in Hetherington, EM (1983) *Handbook of Child Psychology.* New York: John Wiley.

McCubbin, HI and others (eds) (1999) *The Dynamics of Resilient Families.* Thousand Oaks: Sage.

McKendrick, J (1995) 'Poverty in the United Kingdom: the Celtic divide', in Philo, C (1995) *Off the Map: The Social Geography of Poverty in the UK.* London: CPAG.

Middleton, S and others (1995) *Family Fortunes.* London: CPAG.

Morrow, V (1999) *Searching for Social Capital in Children's Accounts of Neighbourhood and Network: Preliminary analysis.* London: LSE Gender Institute.

NCH (2004) *Facts and Figures About Scotland's Children.* Edinburgh.

Page, D (2000) *Communities in the Balance: The reality of social exclusion on housing estates.* York: YPS in association with Joseph Rowntree Foundation.

Pavis, S and others (2000) *Young People in Rural Scotland: Pathways to social inclusion and exclusion.* York: JRF and York Publishing Services.

Pierson, J (2002) *Tackling Social Exclusion.* London: Routledge.

Popay, J and others (2003) 'A proper place to live: health inequalities, agency and the normative dimensions of space', *Social Science and Medicine*, 57, 55–69.

Putnam, R (2000) *Bowling Alone*. New York: Simon and Schuster.

Ridge, T (2002) *Childhood Poverty and Social Exclusion*. Bristol: Policy Press.

Rosenthal, S and others (2003) 'Emotional support and adjustment over a year's time following sexual abuse discovery', *Child Abuse and Neglect*, 27(6), 641–61.

Ross, NJ (2002) *Making Space: Children's social and environmental geographies*. PhD thesis, University of Dundee.

Rutter, M (1999) 'Resilience concepts and findings: implications for family therapy', *Journal of Family Therapy*, 21, 2, 119–60.

Rutter, M and Smith, DJ (1995) 'Towards causal explanations of time trends in psychosocial disorders of young people', in Rutter, M and Smith DJ (eds) *Psychosocial Disorders in Young People: Time trends and their causes*. Chichester: Wiley.

Saleebey, D (ed) (2002) *The Strengths Perspective in Social Work Practice*. Boston: Allyn and Bacon.

Schofield, G (2001) 'Resilience and family placement: a lifespan perspective', *Adoption and Fostering*, 25, 3, 6–19.

Seaman, P (2003) *Connecting Experiences: Young people's family lives as a unifying entity*. PhD thesis, University of Glasgow.

Shapiro, DL and Levendosky, AA (1999) 'Adolescent survivors of childhood sexual abuse: the mediating role of attachment style and coping in psychological and interpersonal functioning.' *Child Abuse and Neglect*, 23, 11, 1175–91.

Sibley, D (1995) *Geographies of Exclusion*. London: Routledge.

Simons, RL (1996) *Understanding Differences Between Divorced and Intact Families*. Thousand Oaks: Sage.

Solomon, Y and others (2002) 'Intimate talk between parents and their teenage children', *Sociology*, 36, 4, 965–83.

Stace, S and Roker, D (2004) *Monitoring and Supervision in 'Ordinary' Families*. York: Joseph Rowntree Foundation.

Titterton, M and others (2002) 'Mental health promotion and the early years: the evidence base: risk protection and resilience.' *Journal of Mental Health Promotion*, 1, 1, 20–33.

Trevillion, S (1999) *Networking and Community Partnership*. Aldershot: Arena.

Valentine, G (1997) '"Oh yes I can" "Oh no you can't": Children and parents' understandings of kids' competence to negotiate public space safely', *Antipode*, 29, 1, 65–89.

Valentine, G (2004) *Public Space and the Culture of Childhood*. Aldershot: Ashgate.

Wilkinson, R (1994) *Unfair Shares: The effects of widening income differences on the welfare of the young*. Essex: Barnardo's.

Wilmott, P and Young, M (1957) *Family and Kinship in East London*. London: Routledge and Kegan Paul.

Index

Titles in the Understanding Children's Lives series

Children and Decision Making
Ian Butler, Margaret Robinson and Lesley Scanlan
2005. ISBN 1 904787 54 1

Children's Perspectives on Believing and Belonging
Greg Smith
2005. ISBN 1 904787 53 3

Children's Understanding of their Sibling Relationships
Rosalind Edwards, Lucy Hadfield and Melanie Mauthner
2005. ISBN 1 904787 48 7

Inclusion of Disabled Children in Primary School Playgrounds
Helen Woolley with Marc Armitage, Julia Bishop, Mavis Curtis and Jane Ginsborg
2005. ISBN 1 904787 66 5

Titles in the Parenting in practice series

Parenting and Children's Resilience in Disadvantaged Communities
Peter Seaman, Katrina Turner, Malcom Hill, Anne Stafford, Moira Walker
2006. ISBN 1 904787 70 3

Monitoring and Supervision in 'Ordinary' Families
The views and experiences of young people aged 11 to 16 and their parents
Stephanie Stace and Debi Roker
2005. ISBN 1 904787 42 8

'Involved' Fathering and Child Well-being
Father's involvement with secondary school age children
Elaine Welsh, Ann Buchanan, Eirini Flouri and Jane Lewis
2004. ISBN 1 904787 24 X

Parenting Programmes and Minority Ethnic Families
Experiences and outcomes
Jane Barlow, Richard Shaw and Sarah Stewart-Brown, in conjunction with REU
2004. ISBN 1 904787 13 4

Other titles published for the Joseph Rowntree Foundation by NCB

Reuniting Looked After Children with their Families
A Review of the Research
Nina Biehal
2006. ISBN 1 904 787 64 9

Young People, Bereavement and Loss
Disruptive Transitions?
Jane Ribbens McCarthy with Julie Jessop
2005. ISBN 1 904787 45 2

Understanding What Children Say
Children's experiences of domestic violence, parental substance misuse and parental health problems
Sarah Gorin
2004. ISBN 1 904787 12 6

It's Someone Taking a Part of You
A study of young women and sexual exploitation
Jenny J Pearce with Mary Williams and Cristina Galvin
2003. ISBN 1 900990 83 0

Listening to Young Children
The Mosaic approach
Alison Clark and Peter Moss
2001. ISBN 1 900990 62 8

To order these titles, or any other title published by NCB, call +44 (0)20 7843 6087, email booksales@ncb.org.uk or visit www.ncb-books.org.uk